Growth
Management

growth management

issues, techniques and policy implications

LAWRENCE B. BURROWS

THE CENTER FOR URBAN POLICY RESEARCH
RUTGERS UNIVERSITY
BUILDING 4051 / KILMER CAMPUS
NEW BRUNSWICK, NEW JERSEY 08903

Lawrence B. Burrows is an Associate with the economic consulting firm of Gladstone Associates. A member of their Miami office, he is responsible for the firm's general and growth management planning. He is involved also with market analysis, real estate evaluation, environmental-economic impact analyses, and cost-revenue studies for both the public and private sectors. While pursuing undergraduate and graduate urban planning degrees from Rutgers University and the University of Pennsylvania, respectively, Mr. Burrows was a research assistant at the Center for Urban Policy Research, where his responsibilities included examing the realities of inner city housing costs, investigating effective neighborhood preservation programs, and analyzing alternative transportation financing mechanisms.

Cover design by Francis G. Mullen
Copyright, 1978, Rutgers—The State University of New Jersey
All rights reserved.
Published in the United States of America
by the Center for Urban Policy Research,
New Brunswick, New Jersey 08903

Library of Congress Cataloging in Publication Data

Burrows, Lawrence B
  Growth management.

  Bibliography: p.
  1. Cities and towns—United States—Growth—Management.
2. Suburbs—United States. 3. City planning—United
States. 4. Zoning—United States. I. Title.
HT123.B85   309.2'6'0973   77-24034
ISBN 0-88285-043-1

Contents

Preface

There are specific topics which, in microcosm, bring together many of the strands of a whole society. The pressures at work in responding to the problems involved in these topics both in implementing and retarding their resolution, provide a unique insight into the strains of our time. In many ways, the subject of growth controls is a prime exemplar of this species. Grouped under this rhubric are all the environmental concerns which are increasingly prominent: the natural limits of land-holding capacity, the trade-offs between intensive land use, and the physical limitations of earth and space.

But these elements, while far from easily defined, are much more finite than the particulars at the other end of the spectrum that of the character and individual substance and way of life, which revolve around the level of intensity of land use. For example, as we near the end of the twentieth century, an increasing demand is heard for a return to a simpler, more bucolic environment. Just as the suburb replaced the city as the prime locational target so the suburb in turn finds it very difficult to compete against the lures of the countryside. The drive toward exurbia, and with it greater levels of decentralization—if not socialatomization—becomes a dominent theme, at least for the affluent.

Lodged precariously between these poles are innumerable other parameters that must be reconciled. To name just a few is to slight the vigor of the many, but given that risk, let me mention at the very least the aspirations for *lebensraum* of minority groups seeking their place in the suburban sun; of the new home aspirant who finds that land costs make the most potent of rewards in our society, the private home, a more and more difficult target; of people who have bought land under the presumption that they can build on it in a fashion which will maximize its value only to have value dissipated by local authorities desperate to minimize development; of the older home occupant dismayed by the taxes reflective of growth and no growth.

All these and many other elements are at work within the simple title of Growth Control. How are these elements to be reconciled and yet provide a modicum of equity for the several players both within current times and the future? It is this very important question to which this work is addressed. In it, Larry Burrows, our former student and colleague, provides the crucial tools and methods of planning, of allocation technique, and the like. The resolution of the long-range philosophical and political questions must remain for later workers—within a society less irresolute than our own.

GEORGE STERNLIEB
Center for Urban Policy Research

Acknowledgments

I am especially appreciate of the support of the Center for Urban Policy Research for this research effort, which has spanned my graduate work at the University of Pennsylvania to my present responsibilities with Gladstone Associates. In this regard, I wish to thank Dr. James W. Hughes for initially envisioning the project, Dr. Robert W. Burchell for continually backing my efforts—especially at critical junctures, Stepen R. Seidel for thoughtfully critiquing initial drafts, and Dr. George Sternlieb for his encouragment to publish the study. Their collective impact immeasurably strengthens the book.

Other people have given freely of their time. While at the University of Pennsylvania, I received enlightened guidance and encouragement from Professor Ann Strong. Her ideas regarding the book's structure and content added an important element of cohesion. Similarly, the genius of Professor Jan Krasnowiecki is manifest throughout, challenging conventional wisdom and improving our understanding of land use controls. As lawyers and planners they have demonstrated a unique ability not to be intimidated or confined by the law, but rather to use it to shape more responsive planning programs.

Since leaving the university, my colleagues at Gladstone Associates have been particularly generous in affording me the time to finish this analysis and in enabling me to draw upon their extensive land development experience.

As with any comparable undertaking, the typing demands were enormous. The Center's typing staff—Joan Frantz, Anne Hummel, and Lydia Lombardi—typed initial and revised drafts. I am especially grateful to Diana Dempsey for her patience and long hours in readying the final version. I would like to thank Kathleen Agena and Joseph P. Zimmerman for editing the manuscript, Margaret P. Roeske for her fine proofreading, and Barry O. Jones, the Center's Director of Publications, for guiding the book through to publication.

All these people are responsible for improving the content of the book; any errors, omissions, and misinterpretations remain my own.

L.B.B.

Introduction

Chapter One:
Introduction

The legacy of Daniel Burnham endures through his oft-quoted credo, "Make no little plans; they have no magic to stir men's blood." However, given the complexity of urban and environmental problems facing planners today, Burnham's motto, reinterpreted for today, might well be "make no little plans; in fact, don't make any plans at all."

As the country moves further into the post-industrial era, the philosophical and technological underpinnings that fostered this transition are being reevaluated. Limitless energy, abundant open space, and an unsaturated environment are no longer being perceived as infinite quantities. For years economic and physical expansion was considered analogous with increasing opportunity, heightened social mobility, and rising affluence. Today, it is inconceivable that these pursuits can be continued without first assessing their impacts. These latent trends are becoming more visible, questioning relatively unconstrained expansion, challenging the sacrosanct American growth ethic. While there has always been periodic antigrowth sentiment, its current appeal and permeation in all levels of society indicate a profound change in attitude. As William Reilly aptly put it:

> A new mood in America has emerged that questions traditional assumptions
> about the desirability of urban development. The motivation is not
> exclusively economic. It appears to be a part of a rising emphasis on human
> values, on the preservation of natural and cultural characteristics that make
> for a humanly satisfying living environment.[1]

In the course of the twentieth century, the United States has assimilated
growth first in urban centers and then in their outlying metropolitan regions.
This twin dynamic resulted in a population concentration on a macro level.
These centripetal and centrifugal movements have substantially altered the
structure of American society. Today, the critical mass of American society lives
outside the inner cities. At the turn of the century, every six out of ten persons
lived in rural areas. Three-quarters of a century later, the population of the
suburban rings exceeds that of the central city by a four to three margin.[2]

Similarly, there has been a concomitant movement of industrial and
commercial enterprises to the suburbs. Whatever the causative factors—more
space, less cost, proximity to labor force, minimized social and environmental
consequences—today, the majority of metropolitan jobs are contained in the
suburbs. This almost wholesale flight from urban areas has placed enormous
burdens on the city itself, as well as the outlying portions of the metropolitan
area accommodating this migration. The city has been left with a
disproportionate number of residents needing high levels of public services: the
young, the elderly, and the poor. Combined with the gradual erosion of the
city's tax base, this manifests in a strain on extant services or the elimination of
services altogether.

The suburban problem is just as acute. To accommodate this residential,
commercial, and industrial influx, vast amounts of agricultural lands are being
converted for urban land uses. The Environmental Protection Agency has
documented that on a national scale approximately 4,000 acres of agricultural
land are provided daily for this transformation. Over the course of a year, this
translates to a conversion of 1.5 million acres.[3] While this may not seem
dramatic when measured against the 440-odd million acres of American
cropland, the unfortunate fact is that a good portion of this converted land is
often prime agricultural or unique environmental land.

Aside from the erosion of agricultural land, the suburbanization dynamic has
prompted untimely, discontinuous development. The developer's search for
cheap land laced with infrastructure has created a series of problems on the
urban fringe: unbalanced growth between types of uses; an inability to provide
public services commensurate with development; poor quality of services due to
rapid growth; increased property tax rates to meet the capital costs of service
demands; and development of negative policies concerning social, racial, and
metropolitan solutions.[4]

These geographic and demographic forces have catalyzed new attitudes toward community growth in the form of growth controls—attempts by suburban entities to limit the magnitude and placement of residents within their jurisdiction.

Whether this movement represents what Anthony Downs describes as the "issue-attention cycle" or a more fundamental change of public attitudes, the emerging issues are not going to easily fade away; they cut across too many diverse and competing interests.

But at a macroregional level, severely restricting growth is not a viable alternative. Despite the publicity of the zero population movement, those individuals who will be the major housing consumers over the next ten to fifteen years have already been born. The 46 percent increase in the 25 to 34 year-old age group (see Exhibit I) will substantially tax the nation's varied housing markets. And varied housing markets they will be. Increased household size, or what one prominent observer calls the "dissolution of the modular household,"[5] will focus attention on the relatively small-sized, adult-oriented households not in the child-rearing stages. These shelter needs will translate into a demand for nonconventional housing typified by apartments, townhouses, and other higher density structures.

EXHIBIT I
U.S. POPULATION BY AGE, 1970-1980 (Projected)*

Age	1970	1980	1970-1980 Change Number	Percent
Under 15	57,889	52,970	(4,919)	(8.5)
15-24	36,495	41,228	4,733	13.0
25-34	25,293	36,962	11,669	46.1
35-44	23,142	25,370	2,228	9.6
45-54	23,310	22,406	(904)	(3.9)
55-64	18,664	21,083	2,419	13.0
65 and over	20,084	24,051	3,967	19.8
Total	204,877	224,070	19,193	9.4

* (in thousands)
Source: U.S. Census, *Current Population Reports,* Series P-25.

The resolution of these baseline trends within a broader context of antigrowth will not be easy. While tendencies toward residential diversity are not new, their present magnitude is unprecedented. "They have gained increasing force in suburbia as growth pressures multiply, as the number of non-modular households bulks larger, and as the critical mass of jobs and services located there provides a stronger rationale for more and varied, residential development."[6]

While valid antigrowth arguments persist, the suburbs cannot turn to environmental and fiscal constraints in an effort to exonerate themselves from some level of responsibility. An enlightened public policy regarding these issues recognizes that it is not merely a matter of limiting growth, but rather developing strategies to rationally accommodate it. Unfortunately, most municipalities are inadequately prepared to satisfactorily assimilate future population. Subsequently, they feel threatened at the prospect of doing so. Vanished open space, high-density development, increased taxes, and a variety of other social, fiscal, and environmental factors have congealed into a new nongrowth ethic. This manifests in a set of negative land use controls. Minimum lot sizes, ultimate population ceilings or a moratorium on development reflect this attitude. Yet, not all growth is bad. What is needed is some form of managed growth strategy. Realistically, this would give a municipality or other governing agency the capacity to time and sequence development. The need is to develop comprehensive programs designed to channel growth into developmentally ripe areas, commensurate with the jurisdiction's ability to provide the necessary services. Within this context growth management can be defined as a program designed to "control or influence the rate, amount, or geographical pattern of growth within one or more local jurisdictions."[7] Three generic forms have emerged: Control over the amount of growth; land availability; and the location and adequacy of facilities servicing the growth. While all aim toward similar goals, their approach varies.

Controlling the amount of growth or restricting the number of individuals or homes placed in an area has a direct limiting effect. The smaller the numbers, the less is the need for land, housing or municipal services. Three mechanisms have been designed to achieve this result: moratoria, annual permit limitations, and cap rates. The first two are geared toward the housing element—either by refusing to issue the necessary building, water or sewer permits, or simply setting an annual quota. The cap rate differs in that it works by placing a ceiling on the number of inhabitants that can live in an area. In other words, the former curbs population by controlling housing supply while the latter restrains housing by limiting population.

Controlling land availability has an indirect effect on growth by minimizing the amount of developable acreage. Again, the less land amenable to development, the fewer the number of inhabitants. Open space acquisition programs, exclusive or nonresidential zones—agriculture, industrial or commercial—rigid annexation policies or the creation of urban service areas achieve this purpose. While the first three exclude residential uses, urban service areas do not differentiate by use; rather they geographically restrict growth by cordoning off sectors to which all types of expansion are channeled. Similar to this concept, but taking it one step further, is a plan which directs growth via placement of infrastructure.

The location and adequate facility policy is another indirect method of regulating growth. The population of a given area cannot be increased if the necessary services—water, sewer, roads—to sustain this population are not or cannot be provided. Exactions, in the form of builder, money, facility or land contributions, are the municipality's way of making the developer pay for the imbalances he may potentially create by increasing the load on the city's service capacities. Another type of public facility policy is more flexible, in that the municipality agrees to provide the requisite services but over a specified period of time. Again, while neither policy directly limits population, they can channel, and even in some cases restrict, development.

Although facility policies can be implemented at all jurisdictional levels, the preponderance of attention has been on municipalities. They have the power to enact such controls and, if necessary, defend them in court. While caution is necessary in areas where local policies significantly interfere with demographic and market dynamics, regional management is not a panacea either. Though there is generalized agreement that land use policy would improve if certain controls were shifted to a higher level of authority, a broader approach may in fact reinforce existing problems. Some municipalities have taken the position that, as part of a regional area, any obligation they may have had to provide for a particular use was waived upon its existence in another part of the region. In other words, as the area in which to assess land use and housing enlarges, it becomes increasingly more difficult to specify between municipal and regional responsibility. Regionalism may justify present social and housing stratification (resulting from current exclusionary zoning practices) rather than reform the existing restrictive land use orientation.[8]

Increased growth has affected all levels of government. However, this study will focus on the municipal-county level, for the greatest concentration and impact of development remains there. In this effort I will attempt to define and analyze the variety of tools municipalities can and have embraced in an effort to manage their growth. Exhibit II indicates the type and location of the growth control systems to be examined.

While this is not meant to be an exhaustive study, the fifteen or so techniques spread over thirty-five locales in twelve states do represent a full complement of the types of programs that have been implemented. Exhibit III shows the regional dispersion of these tools based on a survey of 400 developers. The results of the survey, conducted by the Center for Urban Policy Research

EXHIBIT II
TYPE AND LOCATION OF GROWTH CONTROL SYSTEMS

	Open Space			Zoning		Interim Controls		Division of Land		Second Generation				Total
	Fee Simple	Easement	Tax Relief	Exclusive Zones	Special Permit	Planning Pause	Permit Moratoria	Annexation	Exaction	Urban Service Area	Cap Rate	Annual Permit Limitation	Public Facilities	Total
California														
Petaluma					X			X				X		3
San Jose													X	1
Livermore								X					X	2
Milpitas													X	1
Pleasanton			X											1
Palo Alto												X		1
Sacramento County				X						X				2
Colorado														
Boulder	X	X		X					X		X			5
Pitkin County												X		1
Connecticut														
Enfield												X		1
Milford													X	1
Florida														
Boca Raton	X					X					X			3
St. Petersburg											X			1
Pinellas County									X	X			X	3
Manatee County													X	1
Dade County									X					1
Maryland														
Montgomery County	X		X										X	3
Prince Georges County	X		X											2
Howard County				X										1

	Open Space			Zoning		Interim Controls		Division of Land		Second Generation				Total
	Fee Simple	Easement	Tax Relief	Exclusive Zones	Special Permit	Planning Pause	Permit Moratoria	Annexation	Exaction	Urban Service Area	Cap Rate	Annual Permit Limitation	Public Facilities	
Minnesota														
Brooklyn Park													X	1
Twin Cities										X				1
Missouri														
St. Louis													X	1
New Jersey														
Marlboro												X		1
New York														
Ramapo		X			X	X							X	4
Sands Point					X									1
New Castle												X		1
Clarkstown													X	1
Oregon														
Salem				X				X						2
Eugene										X				1
Springfield										X				1
Marion County								X						1
Pennsylvania														
Bucks County				X										1
Virginia														
Richmond				X										1
Fairfax County							X						X	2
Loudoun County			X						X					2
Totals	2	2	4	6	3	2	2	4	4	5	3	6	13	56

Source: Survey done by Center for Urban Policy Research. Summer, 1976.

(CUPR), show little regional differentiation, although developers in the Northwest and West are more prone to run into growth resistance. This absence of significant variation suggests that growth controls are more a function of intrametropolitan dispersal than of any major regional shifts.

EXHIBIT III
REGIONAL PERCENTAGE DISTRIBUTION OF BUILDERS ENCOUNTERING GROWTH CONTROL ORDINANCES

Type of Mechanism	Northeast[1]	South[2]	Northcentral[3]	West[4]
Sewer Moratorium	52.2	45.8	44.4	50.0
Adequate Public Facility Ordinances	38.1	22.3	28.6	35.5
Population Caps and Annual Permit Limitations	6.8	1.5	4.6	13.2

1. Sample size equals 118.
2. Sample size equals 117.
3. Sample size equals 61.
4. Sample size equals 75.
Note: Numbers will not add to 100.0 due to the multiplicity of responses.
Source: Center For Urban Policy Research, Winter 1976 Survey of Homebuilders.

Further empirical investigations better identify the dimensions of growth management strategies. Returning to the CUPR survey, it was found that the most frequently used mechanism was the moratorium (See Exhibit IV). Almost half of the builders had experienced this particular restriction. Programs relating to the availability of public services was the next most prevalent tool, encountered by nearly one-third of the respondents. The use of absolute ceilings, such as cap rates or annual permit limitations, occurred in only 6 percent of the survey cases, and does not appear to have spread as rapidly as the other control devices.

These findings are also supported in a survey of the planning agencies.[9] Using information based on the agency's perception of their management program, Exhibit V illustrates that the moratorium was perceived to be most effective. This is not surprising, for the technique has an immediate, direct and highly visible impact. Unfortunately, it is not a permanent solution for development management for it is only an interim, short-term remedy, one which does not affect requests (for sewer, water, building permits, etc.) that are currently in the pipeline (see the chapter on Interim Controls).

EXHIBIT IV
*DEVELOPERS' EXPERIENCE WITH
GROWTH CONTROL ORDINANCES*

Type of Mechanism	Percent Experienced[1]
Sewer Moratorium	49.0
Adequate Public Facilities Ordinances	32.1
Population Caps and Annual Permit Limitations	5.8

1. Based on a sample size of 400, this represents the percentage of respondents that have encountered the specific technique. Several respondents reported experiences with more than one type of control mechanism.
Source: Center for Urban Policy Research, Winter 1976 Survey of Homebuilders.

Consistent with the developer's response, the next most effectively rated tool was the adequate facilities ordinance—conditioning development to the provision of adequate infrastructure capacity. No doubt the New York Appellate Court's upholding of the Ramapo case[10] has fostered increased use of this type of ordinance. Interestingly, traditional planning tools—zoning, subdivision, and open space programs—were found to be least effective, supporting the emergence of the "expanded" plans discussed later.

In both Exhibits IV and V the lack of large-scale acceptance or use of the annual permit limitation is evident. In the same way that the *Ramapo* decision has promulgated the adequate facilities ordinance, the absence of the permit limitation is probably attributable to the only recent circuit court's validation of the tool in *Petaluma*.[11] "While judicial intervention, particularly in regard to exclusionary zoning matters, is a welcome departure from the court's historical reluctance to meddle in local land use matters, the court cannot infringe upon the planner's ability to pursue goals, choose tools, and apply technical expertise

EXHIBIT V
*PERCEIVED EFFECTIVENESS OF DEVELOPMENT
TIMING TOOLS AND TECHNIQUES*

Type of Mechanism	Effectiveness Index[1]	Very Effective	Moderately Effective	Slightly Effective	Not Effective	Total
Moratoria[2]	1.73	69	47	17	7	140
Adequate Public Facilities Programming[3]	1.75	13	14	5	-	32
Urban Service Areas	1.77	8	11	3	-	22
Division of Land[4]	1.95	19	25	10	3	57
Zoning[5]	2.24	21	32	17	12	82
Open Space Programs[6]	2.37	5	10	14	1	30

1. Derived by assigning a score of 1 for a rating of very effective, 2 for moderately effective, 3 for slightly effective and 4 for not effective. The index is the average (mean) score. Thus, the lower the index number, the higher the perceived effectiveness.
2. Includes: Water/sewer hook-ups, subdivision, water/sewer extension, building permits and legislative and administrative zoning moratoria.
3. Includes: Public investment policies and phased growth ordinances.
4. Includes: Subdivision regulations.
5. Includes: Agricultural and large-lot (over two acres) zoning.
6. Includes: Public land management and preferential tax policy regimes.

Source: David J. Brower et al., *Urban Growth Management Through Development Timing*, pp. 106-107.

in solving growth problems." Essentially the issue becomes not "what should we do" but rather "how far do we have to go."

Needless to say, the emergence of these management strategies has caused quite a stir in many quarters. Citing legal infringements, exclusionary tendencies, defiance of market dynamics and other adverse implications, many participants and observers of the development process have legally and intellectually challenged the enactment of growth control plans. As a result, otherwise obscure localities have obtained national prominence in their application and defense of their management programs. Notwithstanding valid criticisms, growth control programs can be a very useful instrument—primarily due to their integration of planning tools backed, in many cases, with a financial commitment. This more comprehensive scope, monetarily reinforced, takes the conventional master plan a step further. A management strategy has teeth, it is action oriented.

Because growth is going to continue and because it will be experienced primarily in suburban and nonmetropolitan areas, it is necessary to examine why communities react negatively to encroaching urbanization. In an analysis of thirteen communities enacting some form of management program,[12] the authors found that the principal motivation for enacting management was to hold down municipal servicing costs. Other salient reasons address the desire to maintain the existing life style, to preserve environmentally sensitive lands, protect prime agriculture lands, and to provide low- and moderate-income housing. The previously mentioned survey of planning agencies further corroborates these findings.[13] As indicated in Exhibit VI, 84 percent of the respondents claimed minimizing the service imbalance as their primary motivation in enacting such controls. Three-quarters of those surveyed indicated that the program was adopted in order to reduce sprawl and to protect the environment. In two-thirds of the cases, preserving open space was the primary motive for adoption of a management program, while 55 to 60 percent said their programs addressed maintenance of community character and local amenities. Less than one-third were concerned with checking the population growth rate, with half this amount concerned with actual resident limitation. What all this suggests is that most communities responding were committed to the management, not cessation, of growth. However, as we will see later, the prevalence of cap rates or even moratoria clouds this conclusion.

Nevertheless, regardless of motives, it is essential to point out that even if an effective management program can be developed, it is not a cure-all, for growth management is largely a suburban phenomenon. It addresses the conversion of thus far undeveloped land. Hard issues face the variety of experts (and not so expert) dealing with urban problems. Disinvestment, abandonment, and a variety of other problems are outside the scope of such a program. Yet, they are just as central to the planning profession as suburban problems are for planning in a diverse discipline. A growth control system does not replace planning; rather it

EXHIBIT VI
*OBJECTIVES OF GROWTH MANAGEMENT
STRATEGIES*

Objective	Percent Responding To the Varied Objectives
Provision of Adequate Services	84
Reduction of Urban Sprawl	78
Environmental Protection	78
Preservation of Open Space	66
Preservation of Community Character	60
Preservation of Local Amenities	55
Reduction of Traffic Congestion	53
Improvement of Financial Stability	44
Prevention of School Overcrowding	38
Control of Population Growth Rate	30
Reduction of Private Speculation	26
Protection of Property Values	19
Control of Housing Costs	17
Limitation of Population	14
Lowering of Tax Rates	10
Other	12

Source: Brower et al., *Urban Growth Management Through Development
        Timing*, p. 109.

is one part of a larger system which recognizes the diversity of human, economic and environmental activity.

Perhaps the major fault with present growth management plans is that they have been developed in response to a particular problem with little consideration given to the side effects of the system's operation. To complicate this, few growth management programs engage in any monitoring or annual reviews and, thus, cannot check on the system's effectiveness.

Another drawback to effective growth management lies in undue suspicion of developers or, more generally, of development. Development needs to be examined on its own merit, not condemned by vague suspicions. This attitude is one source of the municipality's desire to burden the developer with as many service costs as possible. While legally validated, and many times justified, exactions in the form of capital, monetary, or service donations increase the cost of housing, prohibiting construction of low or moderately priced structures. At the same time, a variety of environmental controls make it more difficult to build on a scale which can be more environmentally sensitive. Ironically, these added constraints discourage economies of scale which would allow for the packaging of a quality product, including the provision of low-income housing.[14]

Addressing the low-income housing issue, many agencies have developed quantitative standards saying that, for every x units of housing built, the developer needs to provide y units of low-income shelter. Recognition of the need for low-income housing, particularly by suburban communities, is welcome. However, placing the burden singularly on the developer to build these units cannot absolve the municipality of its responsibility. A somewhat more affirmative approach is needed.

Probably the most renowned management system is the one in Ramapo, New York.[15] The conditioning of development to the town's ability to provide the requisite services has been duplicated across the country. While this can be an effective way to accommodate development, particularly since Ramapo agreed to provide the needed facilities itself over an eighteen-year period, many localities attempt to link development to service provision without controlling the service that development depends upon. It is an arrogant municipal policy which tells a developer he cannot build yet does not have the capacity to provide the needed services itself.

The other nationally recognized development tool is the annual permit limitation. The recent circuit court's upholding of the Petaluma plan[16] has catalyzed other similar municipal efforts. While being criticized for its seemingly arbitrary 500-building permit limit, Petaluma's decision might not be as restrictive as it appears. Considering the variety of land use tools a municipality has, nonarticulated quotas—supported by minimum lot sizes—are just as devastating as setting an arbitrary number. At least with the Petaluma program, the quota was out in the open, exposed to public debate. Denying one developer a project and approving another one produces the same result as assigning a numerical limit, yet the former is often not open to public scrutiny.[17]

Even these past cases do not reveal the true dimensions of a managed growth strategy. While controlling growth is not a new phenomenon,[18] what is different about the current techniques is their integration of traditional fragmented tools into a development package. Zoning, subdivision, and open space programs are being combined with capital improvement plans in an effort to manage development. This public investment initiative puts the developer on notice as to where the municipality would like development to occur, with services preceding actual development. Ideally, these systems should illustrate which choices or decisions accord with the overall plan and what would be the impact if certain courses of action were pursued. Unfortunately, the state of the art has not developed to that point yet.

In this study, the numerous approaches to guiding growth will be discussed. Some methods have been around for a long time—open space procurement, zoning, moratoria, and subdivision. Newer thrusts, or "second generation" techniques, expound upon traditional instruments and encompass urban service boundaries, cap rates, annual permit limitations, and adequate public facility programs. Important program elements will be discussed, analyzed, and linked to case studies in an effort to provide a solid understanding of the technique, its issues, and application. The first section will deal with conventional planning tools: first, open space as a growth management system, followed by zoning, moratoria, and subdivision control plans. These underpinnings set the format for the newer methods. "Second generation" techniques will be presented beginning with urban service boundaries, to cap rates, through annual permit limitations, and concluding with adequate public facility programs. A legal section follows discussing not only case law and constitutional issues, but also how far a municipality must go in planning for growth. Finally, a conceptional growth management model will be presented.

The impending clash of demographic, fiscal, and environmental trends will define the context within which a growth management strategy must operate. It is hoped that this analysis will aid in the resolution of these issues.

NOTES

1. William Reilly, ed., *The Use of Land: A Citizen's Policy Guide to Urban Growth* (New York: Thomas Y. Crowel Company, 1973), p. 17.

2. For a discussion of suburbanization see: James Hughes, "Suburbanization and Growth Controls," 422 *The Annals of the American Academy of Political and Social Science* 61, 63 (1975).

3. United States Environmental Protection Agency, *Control of Erosion and Sediment Disposition From Construction of Highway and Land Development,* (Washington: 1971), p. 11.

4. Robert Freilich, "Development Timing, Moratoria, and Controlling Growth," *Management and Control of Growth*, Vol. II, edited by Randal Scott, (Washington, D.C.: Urban Land Institute, 1975), p. 362.

5. George Sternlieb, "The Future of Housing in New Jersey," *Growth Controls,* edited by James Hughes, (New Brunswick, New Jersey: Center for Urban Policy Research, Rutgers University, 1974), p. 229.

6. Hughes, "Suburbanization," p. 69.

7. Michael Gleeson et al., "Urban Growth Management Systems: An Evaluation of Policy Related Research," *Planning Advisory Service*, Vols. 309 and 310 (Chicago: American Society of Planning Officials, 1975), p. 1.

8. Robert Burchell et al., "Exclusionary Zoning: Pitfalls of the Regional Remedy," Hughes, *Growth Controls*, p. 36.

9. David Brower et al., *Urban Growth Management Through Development Timing,* (New York: Praeger Publishers, 1976), pp. 101-114.

10. Golden v. Planning Board of the Town of Ramapo, 285 N.E. 2d 291 (1972).
11. Construction Industry Association of Sonoma County v. City of Petaluma.
12. See Gleeson, "Urban Growth," p. 3.
13. See Brower, "Urban Growth . . . Development," p. 108-110.
14. Sternlieb et al., "The Future of Housing and Urban Development," 27 *Journal of Economics and Business* 99 (1975).
15. Golden v. Planning Board of the Town of Ramapo, 285 N.E. 2nd 291 (1972).
16. Construction Industry Association of Sonoma County v. City of Petaluma.
17. Jan Krasnowiecki, *Zoning Litigation: How To Win Without Really Losing,* unpublished, University of Pennsylvania Law School, Philadelphia, Pennsylvania, 1975.
18. For instance, a municipal ordinance enacted 300 years ago in Cambridge, Massachusetts, mandated that buildings could not be erected in outlying regions until the interstices were filled in.

Section I
First Generation Techniques

Section I
First Generation Techniques

Twenty years ago, Henry Fagin, discussing development regulation, commented that "until the science of planning invents greatly improved methods for regulating the timing of urban development, many attempts at space coordination must continue to fail—master plans remaining unrealized, zoning ordinances ineffectual and rapidly obsolescing."[1]

Clearly, the limited supply of undeveloped land presents innumerable challenges to decision makers faced with implementation of development strategies. Rapid urbanization with its attendant residential and service demands has spawned disparate growth, inefficient service provisions, encroachment of open space, spiraling taxes, and inequitable housing policies.

To counter these trends municipalities have adopted traditional planning tools. Aimed at bringing order to development, public land acquisition, zoning, and subdivision plans were developed. The conflict arising between dominant socio-economic forces (associated with growth) and municipal fiscal constraints has catalyzed many reconciliation attempts. This section expands upon these measures and illustrates their application.

Chapter Two:
Public Acquisition of Open Space

Public land acquisition is based on the theory that the government has the greatest opportunity to manage and direct growth when the land is publicly held. Indirectly, this strategy is an attempt to minimize growth through controlling developable parcels. By regulating open space, a community's overall land use intensity can be controlled, thus affecting the amount of population that can be assimilated.

Predicated on an overall design, lands particularly susceptible to conversion pressures can be protected through full or partial government acquisition. The attraction of this method is its ability to preserve open space, remove land from development, enhance the overall community aesthetic appeal, and improve marketability of surrounding, but unencumbered, parcels. There are four basic methods for government acquisition of land: simple purchase, easement, tax concessions, and compensable regulations.

The first method represents the outright purchase of title and all associated rights. The main deficiency is its excessive cost. Additionally, this technique has proved ineffective where development is imminent; and, when land can be acquired, it is usually spread throughout the community—prohibiting any contiguous acquisition. These obstructions have prompted use of the easement. This essentially has the same characteristics as the fee approach; however, the governmental agency only partially acquires property interests. Again, the cost of easement, its inability to work where growth pressure is manifest, and the need to specifically delineate the rights and limitations of the governmental interest have minimized its application. This has led to the use of tax incentives which enable a reduction of an owner's tax payments provided the land is left in a relatively undeveloped state. The problem arising here is the unwillingness of individuals to engage in such a program and the cumbersomeness of the associated administrative and bookkeeping details. More importantly, this tool can be self-defeating in that it promotes land development. This ironic twisting occurs when an individual holds the land in a "lessened" state—paying reduced taxes until the time he can receive the highest offer for the property. The financial rewards accruing in this case often far exceed the tax repayment penalties, so the government actually subsidizes and promotes the conversion process. The compensable approach minimizes this by combining zoning and eminent domain powers. The municipality permanently zones a parcel at a particular use level; however, if at the time the owner wants to sell, his land value is reduced, compensation is received—but the buyer is on notice as to the type of uses allowed. While this solves the development problem, its cost and the difficulty in determining land values on such a large-scale basis reduce its effectiveness.

Recommendations in devising a growth management plan through open space techniques include: (1) combining the program with other management strategies; (2) acquiring a less than fee interest in the land; (3) actively encouraging individual land donations; and (4) encumbering lands where development pressures are not presently manifest.

Simple Purchase

In legal parlance, the outright purchase of a specific parcel is known as fee simple. This technique, enabling the acquiring agency to receive full title and all rights associated to the land, represents a method through which land imminently threatened with development can be temporarily or permanently removed from the market. It is a method most commonly used by governments to protect areas of open space.

Many communities, coming to national attention through their enactment of various growth control plans, have subscribed to this method. Boca Raton, Florida, perhaps best known for initiating an ordinance to set a population cap rate of 100,000, has used fee simple to purchase beachfront property. In another effort to implement its population policy, roughly 74 acres have been purchased (at a price approximating $17 million) which under existing ordinances would have generated 1,300 housing units.[2] Similarly, this direct appropriation method became a major component underlying the Boulder, Colorado growth strategy.

Expansive employment opportunities, primarily associated with the University of Colorado, and the area's natural beauty lured substantial population to Boulder. An almost twofold increase in population during 1960-1972 endangered the surrounding foothills as vacant land was developed to meet the demands of a growing population. Rapid conversion engendered public concern in a city that has a long history of preservation efforts.[3] This resulted in a policy directed at preserving scenic areas, clustering development, and encompassing the city in greenbelts physically isolating Boulder from its surrounding municipalities.

Beginning in 1964, a special bond issue was passed, allowing the city to purchase a threatened mesa. This effort was reinforced when four years later, pursuant to a conference and civic group pressures for a greenbelt program, a measure earmarking 40 percent of a 1 percent sales tax to secure the foothills section was overwhelmingly passed. Within a month and a half after the greenbelt program's initiation, 1,000 acres had been obtained, supplemented with an additional 1,800 acres by 1972.[4]

To facilitate acquisition, an advisory committee on open space was established. Using a point-ranking system composed of cost and intensity of use factors, a set of purchase priorities was developed. The approximately $600,000 annual sales tax revenue was budgeted to purchase, in ranking order, the mountain backdrop, scenic mesas, creeks and steams, lakes and connecting links.[5]

Despite progress, procurement was financially constrained. Subsequently, the initial sales tax levy was augmented (1971) when, again by ballot, provisions were made to float $5.5 million in revenue bonds. However, the continual need for increased funds, despite concerted municipal efforts, thwarted the greenbelt effort and, in a broader context, underscores an inherent disadvantage in this approach: *the excessive costs.* Anticipating and planning for open space needs, before development pressure spirals land costs, can ease the burden on municipal economies.[6] Reluctancy to commit monies or purchase land soon enough, before development pressure threatens, undermines the fee simple technique. However, even with enlightened public direction, the financial commitments necessitated to control growth are prohibitive. An open space plan for the nine-county San Francisco Bay Region approximated $1.25 billion.[7] Fulfillment of Boulder's objectives would cost a staggering $15-26 million, a long way to go at the annual budgeted level of $600,000.

Once governmental intentions to manage growth become clear, land values in the area become artificially inflated. This inflation is then heightened through speculation, premised on the expectation of high condemnation awards. To complicate matters, willing sellers frequently do not exist, necessitating condemnation proceedings. The ensuing legal action is frequently more costly than voluntary settlements. The combination of these factors further drains already limited acquisition funds.

Furthermore, governmental appropriations do not end after procurement. Maintenance and the removal of the parcel from the tax rolls are additional expenses. Mere acquisition of land by one governmental agency does not assure continuation of the agency's growth management policy. Vast acreages of undeveloped land have been transformed into highways and other pro-growth uses by competing governmental agencies.[8] Additionally, when it is used as the single regulatory mechanism in areas of impending expansion, the fee simple process is powerless against spiraling land costs.

Easements

The acquisition of an easement provides for selected property rights on a given parcel. Through easements, development can be controlled without the high costs of the fee simple process. The easements obtained can be either positive, giving the public certain rights of usage, or negative, limiting those uses.

The excessive cost, maintenance, and tax loss associated with outright purchase are overcome in that the nonconveyance of title leaves the land on the tax rolls with the concomitant expense remaining with the owner. Additionally, the easement mechanism arouses less landowner opposition since possession stays with the original owner, and since the land is still productive, the pressure to succumb to speculation is minimized.[9]

Land placed within the easement receives favorable taxation to the extent that the easement reduces the base upon which the tax rate is applied. As William Whyte has noted, land protected through this guarantee enhances the marketability of the undeveloped portions.[10] Financial relief is also attained through a gift of an easement, allowing a personal income tax deduction equal to the fair market value of the donated property rights. Monetary reliefs coupled with the continuation of existing uses on the developed portion of the parcel primarily account for the appeal of this approach.

Because of these advantages, Boulder supports its fee simple program through scenic easements. This tandem strategy is employed to extend the Greenbelt program to areas particularly susceptible to development. Ramapo, New York has engaged in similar easement acquisition.

In pursuit of a policy linking the timing of development with a capital facilities program, some parcels in Ramapo were deemed undevelopable for periods up to eighteen years.[11] To ease the burden resulting from this imposition, various relief mechanisms were established. A development easement acquisition commission was established in 1967 to ameliorate hardships for individuals who own land in developable areas. Accordingly, an affected owner may petition the commission for a reduction of his land's assessed valuation due to the temporary restrictions.

Aside from this reactionary approach—waiting for the aggrieved to petition for relief—the commission is empowered to investigate prime open space areas which would reinforce the town's efforts to enhance the present or potential value of abutting or surrounding development, maintain the conservation of natural or scenic resources, and further the controlled growth and development strategy.[12] After determining that acquiring a given parcel would benefit the overall growth management policy, and after consulting with the appropriate planning, drainage, and recreation agencies, the town contacts the parcel's owner(s) and makes its acquisition interest known. Upon completion of transfer arrangements, the agreement is submitted to the town board for further action. Assuming the action is granted, the new valuation will take into account depreciation in land price resulting from the easement.

Despite their ability to overcome many of the deficiencies arising in the fee simple context, easements have limitations. Analogous to outright buying, less than fee measures have not proven successful in sections where land development pressures exist already. Where these tendencies exist and speculation occurs, easement accession becomes untenable. Although easement costs are a fraction of those for the fee simple method, they can still be prohibitive.

Further restrictions are the lack of flexibility as conditions change and the lack of positive inducements for public use of the site. Specific delineation of rights and limitations are constraining, sometimes outweighing initial acquisition savings. These deficiencies prompted Norman Williams to note that scenic easements "are most successful where they protect against serious dangers, where the land was not subject to strong development pressures and where its normal use was not greatly affected and where the easements were affirmative, rather than negative in chararacter."[13]

While these impingements have not rendered the easement useless, its ability to inhibit conversion has prompted analysis of another measure designed to alleviate inappropriate development—tax concessions.

Tax Concessions

Aside from raising revenue, tax programs can be a tool to develop and shape development policies. The underlying rationale is that tax relief for landowners could counter development pressures. Specifically, "if high taxes on undeveloped land tend to accelerate the movement of land into higher use categories, lower taxes will decelerate this trend."[14] Maryland, in 1956, became the first state to enact a broad-scale tax program aimed at preserving open land. This program has since been paralleled by other states and has even been linked with comprehensive controlled growth programs. Extending the state program, Montgomery County, Maryland created a new "rural zone" classification in 1973. This zoning category, encompassing 40 percent of the county, specifies 5 acres as minimum residential lot sizes, and is designed to hasten rapid expansion. To reinforce this effort, a preferential tax assessment is extended to farmland in this rural zone. Similarly, Prince Georges County, Maryland provides that farmland be taxed not according to the market value but rather its existing farm use worth. Oregon state law expands this idea by automatically providing tax deferment to land devoted exclusively to farm uses. Loudoun County, Virginia is utilizing a state edict which determines farmland taxation according to its present use.[15]

The idea of not taxing land at its "highest and best use" presents formidable barriers to governmental agencies mandated, through state constitutions, to provide uniform and equal tax treatment. The market value of a comprehensively zoned area reflects its highest *potential* use. Thus, taxes on a less intensive application favor future full development at the expense of present owners. This outcome is antithetical to any open space program. It is inconceivable that any long-range management scheme can be sustained in areas where property taxes reflect potentially high development value. To solve this dilemma, Donald Hagman has proposed three methods for modifying property taxation: general directive, tax preference, and tax deferral.[16]

The general directive assumes that current controls placed on the land are finite, if there is no clear evidence to the contrary. Land is *not* valued as if it were free of restrictions, but rather at its present use. Preferential assessment allows land to be valued at its current or permitted use; however, differing from the general directive, it is applied to only select parcels, and there is no requirement that the land remain permanently undeveloped.

However, the serious uniformity and taxation question posed by these methods, including the increased tax burden on surrounding neighbors, makes the tax deferral approach more attractive. Basically, payment of taxes on the portion of market value exceeding the value of the present use is postponed until the land is subjected to a more intensive use. This avoids the uniformity constraint of the state constitutions because the assessment remains unchanged. William Whyte has remarked that tax benefits accruing from tax preferential schemes result not as much from a decrease in assessments but rather by preventing increased valuations.[17]

Enormous benefits arising from speculators holding land in an undeveloped state, paying proportional taxes, and then selling the land at a capital gain has tempered preferential assessments. This "public subsidy," reinforcing the conversion process, has prompted remission clauses to recapture a portion of forgiven taxes. Once land is developed in a manner not consistent with the tax provisions, back taxes become due. The accumulation of deferred taxes for an indefinite period can be excessive; therefore, taxes reduced beyond a certain period, possibly fifteen to twenty years, are not collected.

Criticism against preferential strategies has been voiced by those who question the willingness of individuals to keep their land open in exchange for tax benefits. The discontinuous development which may result is a deterrent to optimal planning.

Facing the reality of development pressures, one commentator has argued that the financial value of selling out to the developers exceeds any deferral scheme that might be offered to a landowner.[18] Furthermore, when enough owners have come within the taxing scheme, the property values of those in contiguous areas would rise, increasing their potential for development. This ironic twisting of objectives is self-defeating:

> (P)referential farm assessment has little overall effect on the pattern and timing of development. Aside from the relatively few holdouts and those few who prefer to farm in the face of much greater returns from sale or conversion, most landowners will yield to the pressure of the market about the time when the land is ripe.[19]

Similarly, echoing this sentiment, a Michigan study concluded that "(i)n this situation, land is not protected from conversion to more intensive use; the only effect is to eliminate the middleman speculator."[20]

Attacking the taxing scheme's basic precept, Marion Clawson has argued that the transition of an agricultural parcel to a more intensive use does not primarily stem from tax pressures but rather highlights the impracticality of maintaining agricultural uses near areas of impending development.[21]

Less direct expenses occur as a result of administrative bookkeeping. The assessor is compelled to keep two sets of valuations for each parcel. Another drawback is that a tenant will have to live on the site a length of time before tax advantages accumulate. In light of liquidity and avoidance of conveyance obstacles, the appeal of deferral is diminished.

In a larger context, the whole array of tax-reducing schemes have come under mounting criticism:

> It seems to be part of our national psychological heritage to consider property tax exemptions as an ideal means of promoting worthwhile enterprises, dispensing charitable aid, furthering social reforms, or showing esteem and gratitude. There is little or no recognition of the fact that many of these objectives could be more effectively, more economically and equitably achieved through a direct and visible subsidy.[22]

Critics argue that a diminished tax base infringes upon a municipality's ability to provide adequate services. While this theory is not without merit, it fails to consider three propositions: (1) some land derives its principal value from less-intensive applications; (2) losses resulting from diminished revenues are recouped on rising valuations on surrounding parcels; and (3) the reduction in municipal revenues is partially offset by lower municipal service expenses.[23]

While there is no empirical evidence to support this last point, one study does document the fiscal advantages of maintaining open space as opposed to development.[24]

Beset with rising employment and residential opportunities, and physiographically constrained, the City of Palo Alto, California sought to minimize these disparities. A prototype cluster development, covering 600 acres, was initiated only to be terminated due to financial difficulties. In the meantime, continual expansion brought about successive development moratoriums, necessitating an environmental design plan for the foothills area. This cost-benefit examination explored alternative design concepts and revealed that of the two dozen patterns simulated, none would yield positive municipal cash flows. Subsequently, it was recommended that the city not pursue foothill development, but purchase the land instead:

> The foothill study results indicate that permitting any development at this time would be a mistake. It is true that residential development at one unit per acre would be less costly than purchase by the city, but market studies indicate that development of this type would proceed at an extremely slow pace. Development of three units per acre would cost 10 percent less cumulatively over 20 years than city acquisitions; but when the bonds were paid off, the continuing cost of residential development would be far higher, even if the city invested a substantial sum in improvement and maintenance of the open land.[25]

However, remitting to a fee-simple solution becomes susceptible to the direct and indirect cost constraints previously detailed. An alternative approach links the police and eminent domain powers for compensable regulations.

Compensable Regulations

As part of a growth management strategy, rigid controls are placed on the land, with owners adversely affected receiving a governmental guarantee equal to the value of their property at the time of the imposition of controls. Such regulatory integration validates confining controls that, without compensation being provided, would be regarded as a taking.

The advantages of this method are:

- The attachment of controls does not require expenditure of large sums of money because compensation is not expended, if at all, until public sale.
- The plan is less costly, for intervening market inflation reduces compensation payments.

— Rational planning is facilitated through flexibility in amending the regulations.[26]

Professors Jan Krasnowiecki and Ann Strong have argued that "compensable regulations are not intended to supersede public acquisition and zoning where these devices make sense as a means of controlling development. They are specifically designed to help meet the objectives of timing and controlling the character of urban growth through the preservation of open space in private hands."[27]

Basically, when the design is set, parcels in the area are valued in a manner resembling "just compensation" computations. These sums are guaranteed by the governmental agency to property owners. Controls mandated through the plan apply to the lands, and to the extent that such impingements depress market value, below the governmentally assured level, the landowner is compensated this difference at the time of sale.[28] This procedure embodies the concept of the 1947 English Town and Country Planning Act, that remuneration is determined at the date of initial imposition.

Under compensable regulations, specifically, if a parcel is assessed at $50,000 but due to the regulations an owner can only receive $30,000, the government, at the time of the sale, pays the seller $20,000 ($50,000-$30,000). The new backing is for $30,000 with this same process repeating until the guarantee is exhausted. Property owners whose sales exceed the insured level are not eligible for compensation, although they can keep any surplus.

Numerous court cases have addressed important elements of this approach in their rulings. In *State ex rel. Willey v. Griggs*,[29] the court invalidated a statute allowing the Arizona highway department to set aside lands needed for future road purposes for a period of up to two years, with acquisition costs set at the initial and not the future existing market value. The court noted that "interference with private property rights prescribed is neither an appropriate nor justifiable means for exercising the State's police power."[30] Similarly, in a Philadelphia case,[31] the judiciary disallowed the city's purchase of property contiguous to a parkway, with resale having been contingent upon preservation restrictions.

However, compensable regulations received support in Minnesota, when the state's supreme court held that, with the provision of compensation payments, eliminating the construction of apartment buildings and other designated building classes was constitutional.[32] This decision received further support in *Kansas City v. Liebi*[33] when the court approved a cordoning from building for business purposes and in proximity to certain streets, with compensation available to parties damaged by such actions. A more recent extension of this philosophy was provided in *City of Kansas City v. Kindle*.[34] Overturning a circuit court ruling, the Missouri supreme court found that a zoning ordinance mandating single-family construction in a subdivision, but providing compensation to those damaged who held multifamily units, was a legitimate exercise of the joint authority of eminent domain and police power.

Despite these divergent judicial rulings, there are significant problems connected with compensable regulations. One such problem arises from the fact that these regulations are not immune to the parochialism associated with conventional zoning. The large-scale nature of guaranteed values necessitates careful administrative scrutiny and could reduce property values on a vast scale.

While compensation may be able to overcome imminent development pressure, the market dynamic can cause precipitous changes in land values. In the case of inflationary land increases the amount of a governmental payment is minimized because the higher real estate values will probably yield more than the government's guarantee. However, a drop in market prices—evidenced in 1973-1974 — forces the government to compensate landowners at artificial, non-market prices. What is lacking are provisions which would identify how much of the loss was occasioned by the regulation as opposed to all other market forces. The absence of such provisions serves to entice speculators who cannot lose on their investment.

The problems arising under the fee simple approach also become acute when this method is implemented on such a large scale. The critical question then becomes to what extent does the governmental action enhance land being valued for condemnation purchases? As Krasnoweicki and Strong have pointed out:

> In compensating for every restriction on land use, it would be unfortunate if all the progress achieved in the last 40 years in bringing courts to recognize the full potential of police power were simply thrown away. While preserving open spaces may demand compensation, there will continue to be, as in the past, a host of planning goals that can properly and effectively be realized through non-compensable regulation.[35]

NOTES

1. Henry Fagin, "Regulating the Timing of Urban Development," 20 *Law and Contemporary Problems* 298, 299 (1955).
2. Michael Gleeson, et al., "Urban Growth Management Systems," *Planning Advisory Service* (Chicago: American Society of Planning Officials, 1975), p. 10.
4. In 1910 Frederick Law Olmstead fashioned the city's initial improvement plan. In 1958, a Blue Line was enacted, limiting areas in which municipal water could be extended. This was followed six years later by a special bond issue appropriating money to purchase a threatened mesa. In 1968, the Greenbelt Program began, supplemented three years later with additional bonding privileges.
4. For an account of the Boulder strategy, see Finkler and Peterson, *Nongrowth Planning Strategies: The Developing Power of Towns, Cities and Regions*, (New York: Praeger Publishers, 1974), pp. 27-42.

5. Environmental Law Society, *A Handbook for Controlling Local Growth* (Stanford, California: Stanford University, 1973), pp. 30-37.
6. However, it is not clear whether governmental entities can condemn land unless the public is going to immediately use it. For further thinking, see: "Preservation Techniques for Open Space," 75 *Harvard Law Review* 1622, 1631-1635 (1962).
7. Clyn Smith III, "Easements to Preserve Open Space Land," 1 *Ecology Law Quarterly* 728, 730 at footnote 12 (1971).
8. Lois Farer, "Preservation of America's Park Lands: The Inadequacy of Present Law," 41 *New York University Law Review* 1093 (1966).
9. William Whyte, *Securing Open Space For Urban America: Conservation Easements,* Technical Bulletin 36 (Washington, D.C.: Urban Land Institute, 1956).
10. William Whyte, *The Last Landscape* (Garden City, New York: Anchor Books, 1968), p. 93.
11. Golden v. Planning Board of the Town of Ramapo, 285 N.E. 2d 291 (1972).
12. See: "Ramapo Development Easement Acquisition Law" reprinted in Charles Little, *Challenge of the Land* (New York: Pergamon Press, 1969), Appendix D.
13. Norman Williams, *Land Acquisition for Outdoor Recreation – An Analysis of Selected Legal Problems* (Washington, D.C.: Outdoor Recreation Resources Commission, 1963), p. 46.
14. "Land Use Planning – New Mexico's Green Belt Law," 8 *Natural Resources Journal* 190, 191 (1968).
15. Currently, over half the states have modified their tax laws to reduce tax burdens on farms. For a further treatment, see: Joseph Henke, "Preferential Property Tax Treatment For Farmland," 53 *Oregon Law Review* 117 at footnote 1 (1974).
16. Donald Hagman, "Open Space Planning and Property Taxation – Some Suggestions" 1964 *Wisconsin Law Review* 628, 638-645 (1964).
17. Whyte, *Last Landscape,* p. 123.
18. Krasnowiecki and Paul, "The Preservation of Open Space in Metropolitan Areas," 110 *University of Pennsylvania Law Review,* 179, 190 (1961).
19. Henke, "Preferential Property Tax," p. 123.
20. "Preferential Property Tax Treatment of Farmland and Open Space Under Michigan Law," 8 *University of Michigan Journal of Law Reform* 428, 446 (1975).
21. Marion Clawson, "Open Space as a New Resource," in *Quality of the Urban Environment,* edited by Harvey Perloff (Baltimore: Johns Hopkins, 1969), p. 170.
22. Mabel Walker, "Loopholes in State and Local Taxes," 30 *Tax Policy* 4 (1963). For a more recent articulation of this see: Stanley Surrey, "Tax Incentives as a Device for Implementing Governmental Policy: A Comparison With Direct Governmental Expenditures," 83 *Harvard Law Review* 705 (1970).
23. Marvin Moore, "The Acquisition and Preservation of Open Space Lands," 23 *Washington and Lee Law Review* 274, 283-284 (1966).
24. Livingston and Blayney, *Foothills Environmental Design Study,* Report 3 to the City of Palo Alto, California, 1970.
25. *Ibid.,* p. 58.

26. Livingston and Blayney, *Foothills,* p. 285.
27. Krasnowiecki and Strong, "Compensable Regulations for Open Space: A Means of Controlling Urban Growth," *Journal of the American Institute of Planners,* Vol. 29 (May, 1963), p. 88.
28. Such a sale is publicly supervised to minimize fraudulent schemes against governmental guarantees. Once the owner has filed proof of sale, the governing agency adjusts the owner's guarantee, reflecting changes in the value of the dollar since the imposition. This variable rate is tied to the Consumer Price Index.
29. 385 P. 2d 174 (1960).
30. *Ibid.* at 177.
31. Pennsylvania Mutual Life Insurance Company v. City of Philadelphia, 88 A. 904 (1913).
32. State ex rel. Twin City Building and Investment Company v. Houghton, 176 N.W. 195 (1920).
33. 252 S.W. 404 (1932).
34. 446 S.W. 2d 307 (1969).
35. Krasnowiecki and Strong, "Compensable Regulations," pp. 97-98.

Chapter Three:
Zoning

Legal validation of zoning did not occur until the *Euclid* decision in 1926,[1] but a municipal ordinance enacted 300 years earlier actually set the precedents for the control policies applicable to today. As a presage to current limitations on discontinuous development, a Cambridge, Massachusetts statute mandated that buildings could not be erected in outlying regions until the interstices were filled in. Despite this vision, pre-Euclidian zoning mainly constituted impositions placed upon building heights and resolution of nuisance claims. With the advent of *Euclid,* accompanied by the Department of Commerce's Standard State and City Planning Enabling Act, zoning rapidly became the most commonly employed development control device. Through charting use districts and regulating building and land plans, land use could be controlled. Specifically, the underlying purpose of zoning is to prevent overcrowding, avoid undue concentrations of population, and to facilitate the adequate provisions of municipal services. This is an indirect strategy in that it impacts population through controlling land use. Basically, four types of zoning regulations have been devised: exclusive zones; denial of multifamily housing; minimum-size standards; and special permits.

The latter establishes a mechanism by which individuals engaging in the building process need to apply for development permission prior to applying for traditional zoning and subdivision review. It is through this regulatory process that prominent management plans have been initiated. The governing agency requires the developer to prove that his plans are compatible with the municipality's overall development plan and that the project can be adequately served by the existing infrastructure, prior to filing for additional review. If the developer is turned down at this stage, he has few immediate recourses.

Under exclusive zoning regulations, residential lands that generate increased population are withdrawn from the market by zoning them for other purposes, such as agricultural, commercial, or industrial. Similarly, zoning for single-family rather than multifamily units serves to restrict intensive development. Regulating the size of lots, floor space, or height of the structures can also effectively limit population density. Taken collectively, these measures indirectly regulate the number of people who can reside in an area by restricting the type and size of the housing provided.

While this subordination to the public good transcends private property right doctrines,[2] what is potentially destructive is that, under the guise of a valid purpose, setting minimum use and size requirements may actually be directed towards prohibiting rather than encouraging specific uses. This deficiency was summarized by the American Law Institute: "The . . . statutes molded assumed that the decision to acquire land for development is made independently of the planning laws and that the purpose of local laws . . . is to *prohibit* (emphasis supplied) undesirable development and not to encourage desirable development."[3]

In addition, zoning may also be used to exclude "unfavorable groups." Recent New Jersey and Pennsylvania exclusionary zoning cases reveal the depth of this problem. However, even assuming well intentioned efforts, zoning's effectiveness as a management tool is questionable. If the goal is to preserve rural character and promote optimal use of infrastructure, how can a system that allows only one house per so many acres enhance rural character? This causes scattered, not harmonious, development. Furthermore, standards are often defined without consideration for physiographic sensitivity. The infrastructure servicing costs for spread development often become prohibitive. All these factors severely restrict responsiveness to differing pressures and to the development capacities of individual parcels. No wonder the planning agency respondents in the survey mentioned in the Introduction found zoning to be a relatively ineffective tool in relation to other strategies.

If some form of management strategy is to be structured around zoning, it should be linked with other management tools, respond to socioeconomic patterns, be sensitive to physiographic characteristics, and encourage cluster development. It is erroneous to assume that a control sufficing in a small area can work in a metropolitan context. We need to recognize that "magnitudes of scale create their own problems and that the limited environmental frame and much greater development intensities ... may require an entirely new intellectual apparatus to undergird the land use allocation system."[4]

The necessity to respond to the demands of increasing urbanization has catalyzed many new regulatory efforts. In this section varied zoning provisions will be explored.

Exclusive Zones

Post World War II suburbanization has prompted governing bodies to "regulate and restrict" the nature, size, and intensity of municipal growth. Following judicial and legislative guidance, methods of regulation were developed "to prevent the overcrowding of land; to avoid undue concentration of population; to facilitate the adequate provision of transportation, water, sewage, schools, parks and other public requirements."[5]

The inability to balance development timing with service provisions, manifesting in soaring infrastructure costs, has broadened the appeal for exclusive districts. As it is commonly applied, this approach withdraws residential areas by zoning them for other uses—agriculture, commercial, industrial—or by zoning exclusively for single-family rather than multifamily or mobile home housing. This method constrains housing supply by allowing only low-density development.

Exclusive districts evolved when "cumulative zoning's" inability to prevent high-density uses from being developed in low-density zones became apparent. Thus, as one method to restrain this trend, ordinances for zoning nonresidential districts were enacted.

Nonresidential Zoning

In order to inhibit premature urban encroachment, outlying areas have been zoned for agricultural use. While such unintensive use will typically permit compatible farm uses or large-lot, single-family homes, conventional subdivisions are usually banned. The use of agricultural sections has also been likened to a "holding zone," limiting development until the immediate demand subsides, then allowing for down-zoning in accordance with future needs.

This device was used in Sacramento County, California where a permanent agrarian zone was created, prohibiting all inconsistent agricultural uses, establishing an agricultural urban reserve area, holding land for foreseeable expansion, and defining a rural-residential portion, according single-family units a minimum of two acres.[6] The latter provision is paralleled in Salem, Oregon, where single-family dwellings are allowed in the exclusive land use zone but subdivisions are forbidden. Though authority for such a policy exists,[7] supplementary aids would lessen the adversity of this imposition. Combining exclusive agrarian zones with open space acquisition techniques could prove effective, conjunctive with the previously delineated advantages and disadvantages. "Temporary zones" with definite development time schedules can also be used to contain sprawl and facilitate the filling in of the intermediate developable areas.

Another group of similar proposals have, as Norman Williams noted, "attempted to bring zoning and planning closer together."[8] Richmond, Virginia identified existing agricultural lands which would eventually be amenable for more intensive development. Three years prior to the scheduled completion of the necessary sewer, road, and water infrastructure facilities, applications for rezoning for higher densities in these areas would be accepted. Aimed at guiding future intensive development, a developer would then have to assure the city that the project was: compatible with existing land use; accessible to major regional thoroughfares capable of handling projected traffic volumes; and adequately serviced with water and sewer in a prime market area, assuring completion as proposed.[9]

A similar strategy was adopted in Bucks County, Pennsylvania. Concerned with scattered development patterns, the county designated four types of land use sectors: (1) developed urban areas; (2) potential development areas, where growth pressures are manifest; (3) rural holding zones, mostly farm and forest, with no strong developmental pressure; and (4) resource protection spots, critical areas.[10] In an attempt to manage present and future development in the second sector, the land use needs anticipated over a five-year period were examined, scheduling supportive facilities to assimilate this expansion. To augment this strategy, developmentally ripe areas were designated as special assessment districts to finance needed services and to counterbalance the reduced tax assessments in the rural zones.

Density development districts are also being considered in Howard County, Maryland. Based on topographic and service criteria, districts would be mapped providing for three levels of density—two, three, and fifteen dwelling units per acre.[11]

Districts can also be zoned exclusively for industrial or commercial uses. Again, with this approach, population growth can be indirectly controlled by removing potential residential areas from the market and by giving industrial or commercial promoters the competitive advantage by facilitating parcel assembly. Richard Cutler has noted that the "construction of residences at random tends to prevent assemblage of large tracts which are needed by modern plants with their one-story structure, large parking lots, and room for future expansion."[12]

However, the court has been slow to respond to such a program. In distinguishing *Roney v. Board of Supervisors of Contra Costa County*[13] from previous invalidations, the court remarked there was nothing inherently arbitrary or unreasonable in exclusive industrial zoning, that a relation to the public health and safety exists in the absense of a finding within a reasonable period of time that the land was not usable for industrial purposes. Analagous to the agricultural setups, exclusive industrial-commercial areas may be invalid as applied. Over-zoning for these uses or zoning the land although it is not adapted for such a purpose within a reasonable time is an illegal application of the police power. Such a procedure was recently litigated when the Township of Mount Laurel zoned 29 percent of its land exclusively for industry (4,121 acres), while only 100 acres were actively being utilized as such.[14]

Flexibility within the planning process is necessary; unbridled authority can threaten the nature and integrity of the planning apparatus. Under the guise of protecting agricultural or open space resources, zoning may actually be used to exclude minorities, the poor, or other "unfavorable" groups. This disception cannot be tolerated for it represents a skewed and discriminatory approach to land use regulation.

Alternative Configurations

The doctrine furthered by the court in *Euclid* protected existing functions from intrusion by discordant uses. "With particular reference to apartment houses, it is pointed out that the development of detached house sections is greatly retarded by the coming of apartment houses, which has sometimes resulted in destroying the entire section for private house purposes; that in such sections very often the apartment house is a mere parasite."[15]

Convinced of Justice Sutherland's argument, regulatory agencies viewed non-detached housing as discordant and segregated it, along with industry, from residential zones. This zoning policy is often perpetuated within the context of a growth control program. Obviously, such a policy serves to limit population. Eliminating such alternative dwelling configurations is an impediment to those who may wish to reside in a given community but who either prefer not to live in a single-family home or cannot afford to do so.[16]

In a study conducted of management strategies only Ramapo, New York was identified as excluding such alternative housing uses. However, if outright exclusion is not a prevalent phenomenon, rigid control over the location of multifamily or mobile homes does occur:

> Some communities, deeming it imprudent to attempt a direct, total exclusion of these housing types from their political boundaries have instead adopted a discrete approach and have employed indirect and subtle means of exclusion.[17]

Augmenting the real or imagined separation justifications, other rationales for segregating these uses are that: (1) nonconventional housing does not pay its own way; (2) property values will be reduced when apartments or mobile homes are introduced; and (3) inhabitants of these housing types are transients who will not contribute to the community. Unfortunately, the advocates of the first proposition are making an unwarranted departure from the historical and legal development of local property taxation. Any implied relationship between services and revenues is not the basis for tax equity. Horizontal equity—that individuals in like circumstances be taxed in a similar manner—forms the "fairness" test in property taxation:

> The germane question in any consideration of a fair share of the property tax, therefore, is whether the property has been appropriately valued in comparison with the values of other properties in the same jurisdiction and not with the degree or type of cost burden the owners or inhabitants of that property place upon the jurisdiction's budget.[18]

Noncoventional or nonstationary housing does not necessarily create a deficit in the municipal budget. The fact that mobile homes sometime pay less than their "fair share" stems from antiquated tax laws, not because of the units themselves. "The point is not that the mobile home owner pays more or less than his counterpart in a permanent home, but that he is taxed differently."[19]

Under existing local taxing methods, a disproportionate amount of revenues collected are used to fund local educational services. The notion that apartment or mobile home dwellers innately produce more children, thus placing a higher burden on the school district, is founded more upon misconceptions than on empirical documentation.

A recent mobile home publication revealed that a typical home owner, a young married with perhaps one child, has a smaller family than its equivalent in a conventional home (2.3 average household size versus 3.2 for an average American household). In fact, approximately 60 percent of mobile home households are without any school age children.[20] Looking at multifamily homes, New Jersey research revealed that alternative unit households produce less children than households in conventional dwellings.[21] While these parameters can vary,[22] the important point is that preconceived suspicions about the alternative housing population should be avoided.

The adverse affliction associated with multifamily or mobile homes has largely arisen from anachronistic characterizations of both the unit and the household. The coming of the twentieth century saw the erection of many cramped quarters, as the cities attempted to assimilate their swelling populations. Consequently, the judiciary and the lay public became familiar with the worst type of multifamily housing because the better apartments did not draw any attention and avoided litigation. Concurrently, this attitude was extended to mobile home owners, tainting this population's reputation.

Though the single family home was popularly romanticized as being exemplary of the American way of life, perceptive observers from early on recognized the fallacy of the "inherent detriment" argument. A year prior to the *Euclid* litigation, one judge questioned, "Do apartment houses *per se* endanger public health, morals or safety. . . . There is not *per se* more danger from fire in apartments than from private houses. . . . Neither are the people who live in apartment houses less moral *per se* than those who live in single dwellings."[23] While unpleasant socioeconomic connotations are possibly understandable in the context of the early 1900s, the stigma that is still attached to these housing types is less justified.

Despite initial judicial antipathy, the Pennsylvania Supreme Court in *Appeal of Girsh*[24] annulled a municipal ordinance that made no provision for apartment buildings as a permissible residential use. Three years later, the same tribunal reaffirmed its position by holding Willistown's failure to provide for apartments as violating the Equal Protection and Due Process clauses of the United States Constitution. Going further than they did in *Girsh,* the divided court noted that

> municipal officials must not only refrain from enacting a zoning ordinance which would bar apartment construction altogether, but they must also refrain from enacting any such ordinance so as to allow apartment construction but necessarily limit it to relatively high-cost construction only.[25]

Picking up on the court's latter wording, increasing apartments' costs—excluding "nondesirable and unsavory tenants," a New Jersey court overturned increased apartment construction cost amendments in a Glassboro zoning ordinance. In *Molino v. Mayor and Council of Borough of Glassboro,* the court held that zoning cannot be used to solve collateral municipal problems.[26]

Similarly, under the "noninfrastructure capability logic," a New York judge held that the Village of South Nyack could not prevent a proposed apartment building on the grounds that the sewage emanating from this building would pollute the Hudson River. Adopting an average versus marginal analytical approach, the court reasoned that all community members contribute to pollution; therefore, it would be unfair to make the proponent bear the sole burden especially when alternative solutions exist. In this instance, municipal resistance to the project was based not on a rational decision process, but rather because the developer came in at the wrong time.[27]

In *Oakwood at Madison, Inc. v. Township of Madison,* the ruling adopted invalidated an apartment provision which, though it allowed 500-700 multifamily units, restricted the number of bedrooms in each unit. Total prohibition of multiunit options was also voided by the same court.[28]

The mobile home case law is anything but unanimous. In two 1969 cases,[29] the judiciary reversed municipal disallowances, finding the restrictions without substantial relation to the public health, safety, welfare, and morals. When stripped of these legal underpinnings and further analyzed, the governing rule hinges upon the property being virtually worthless for anything else. The fact that the sites were located on relatively undesirable lots prompted one writer to comment that "low-income people have a constitutional right to live at high densities on the most worthless land having the worst possible environmental conditions."[30]

This ideology, let them live where nothing else is suitable, contributes to the notion that the units adversely impact property and community values. While in some instances apartment houses or mobile home dwellings may properly be characterized as a discord, this problem cannot be resolved under an exclusionary policy, but rather through a rational inclusionary ordering.

> The question posed is whether the township can stand in the way of the natural forces which send our growing population into hitherto undeveloped areas in search of a comfortable place to live. We have concluded not. A zoning ordinance whose primary purpose is to prevent the entrance of newcomers in order to avoid future burdens, economic and otherwise . . . cannot be held valid.[31]

Addressing the nature of the charge on the previous case, another management mechanism was pursued through the enactment of minimum floor, height, and lot regulations. Sanctioned by the Standard State Enabling Act, many zoning classifications are supported by their tendency to control the intensity of land use. Broadening initial congestion and air and light adequacy provisions, modern lot area requirements are used to protect municipalities from the hazards of rapid land conversion. Analagous to alternative housing exclusions, regulations that limit density place a ceiling on the number of people accommodated per lot, thus indirectly reducing total population.

In an attempt to maintain tax rates as well as property and aesthetic values, size impositions are devised to coordinate land use development. Regulating the size of floors, lots and height can halt, redirect, or guide the nature of impending development.

Minimum floorspace ordinances find more specific justification along the lines of promoting the public safety, welfare, and, especially, health. Consistent with all zoning litigation, such enactments must conform with constitutional and statutory requirements. An illustration of this is afforded in *Lionshead Lake, Inc. v. Township of Wayne*.[32] The 768-square-foot restriction that was sustained afforded the case landmark status. Adopting a peculiarly regional approach, the judiciary contended that Wayne's plan constituted a logical means of favorably controlling population distribution. The outward thrust of the population expansion placed the township in the wave of suburbanization, legitimizing controls to avoid suburban blight.[33] The court was convinced by the expert testimony which documented health standards as a function of space requirements. While the sincerity of the municipality's contention is unclear, criticism of the case's decision has focused on the relationship between the square-foot minimum and the public health. Regulating the former without also regulating family size seems a vague exercise of police power. In other words, requiring that a single-family home must approximate 800-square feet, regardless of whether two, four, six or ten people will live there, is a highly questionable precedent. As such, interior floor area amounts might simply be a veil for exclusionary practices. Justice Oliphant addressed this in his dissent, concluding that

> Zoning has its purposes, but as I consider the effect of the majority opinion it precludes individuals in those income brackets who could not pay between $8,500 and $12,000 for the erection of a house on a lot from ever establishing residence in this community.[34]

Despite this point, the court was able to distinguish the *Lionshead Lake* regulation from previous rulings finding minimum cost requirements unconstitutional.

In discussing the merits of lot size standards, the courts have been circumspect. Typically, they have ruled against such standards in growth areas, recognizing the need to include diverse population brackets. Again, considerations depend upon the reasonableness of the restrictions as applied. Recognizing that the Township of Freehold's almost 1-acre lot size minimum exceeded zoning site regulations in surrounding jurisdictions, the court ruled against the township's stipulation.[35] On the other hand, after considering the adverse ecological and fiscal repercussions upon the town of Sanhornton, the United States Court of Appeals for the First Circuit affirmed a lower opinion upholding a 6-acre minimum size.[36]

In testing the validity of zoning as a growth management tool, the court, in *Board of County Supervisors of Fairfax County v. Carper*[37] held that the 2-acre blanketing of the western two-thirds of Fairfax County was unreasonable, arbitrary, and invalid. In response to the doubling of population during the 1950-1957 period, Fairfax County officials rezoned the western portion of the county from ½-acre standards to 2-acre minimum. Contrary to the county's argument that their actions were based on statutory enabling authority, the court found that:

—Ground water capacity existed to support more development than the 2-acre lot size minimum allowed.
—Increased capabilities in regard to water supply were available.
—Proper sewage facilities could be accorded without jeopardizing public health and safety.

—Demand existed in the area for housing structures requiring less than 2-acre lots.
—The land was not conducive to profitable agricultural use.
—The zoning ordinance did not implement or achieve a reasonable plan of orderly growth.
—The plan's ramifications channeled people into the already densely populated eastern county sector.[38]

Conceding that the 2-acre stipulations were not unreasonable, per se, the court nevertheless reasoned that as applied in Fairfax the regulations were not valid. Not discouraged by its neighboring county's invalidation, Loudoun County, Virginia has recently established two agricultural use districts providing minimum residential lot sizes. In accordance with its plan to preserve the character of existing rural areas, the county has established A-3 (3-acre minimum) and A-10 (10-acre minimum) districts, together encompassing over 80 percent of the county's land area, Loudoun integrates area requirements with preferential taxation schemes. Another Washington metropolitan area county, Prince Georges, has established two large-lot zoning districts: the open space zone and the rural agricultural zone. These regulations are designed to protect environmentally sensitive areas as well as to reinforce rural living character. In a similar approach, Montgomery County, Maryland created a rural zoning district, according 40 percent of the county's land area into 5-acre lots.

The authority to specify height levels is usually derived from the standard state zoning enabling acts. While contradictory rules exist, the general rationale is that height stipulations insure adequate light and air on surrounding parcels, thus reducing fire hazards as well as serving an aesthetic purpose. A more recent program in Boulder, Colorado has incorporated height regulations with a broader program regulating intensity of use, supplemented with simple and easement acquisition provisions. City council action in 1971, specifying 140-foot height limits on structures in dense areas, was vigorously contested. However, fearing obstruction of the mountain backdrop, preserved via the greenbelt plan, the council proposed an even more restrictive height standard of 55 feet (35 feet in low-density residential areas). The proposal was passed, but by a narrow margin. While this is not primarily a growth issue, it is indirectly linked to a management scheme.

However, the purported objectives of many of these regulatory measures have, to date, remained largely unfulfilled. Commenting on Wayne Township's ordinances for regulating minimum floor space, Norman Williams concluded that, fifteen years after enactment, the dramatic growth rate of the municipality experienced in the 1950s has not subsided, that the town has continued to grow at roughly the same pace.[39] Furthermore, lot size standards do not significantly alter growth patterns; rather growth continues in the same pattern but at a slower rate. By forcing builders to use large lots for larger houses, more land is squandered. This tendency proliferates urban sprawl, rather than eliminating it.

In addition, disjointed land planning makes it exceedingly difficult to link any mass transit system into such a low-density pattern. Furthermore, the municipal fisc is continually allocating sums of money to meet the costs of extending sewer and water systems. While this fiscal drain may be lessened as a result of temporarily slowing population growth, the resulting geographic housing displacement produces inefficient line extensions. Hopes of preserving physiographic features are eliminated for identical zoning of all sections of a municipality completely disregards unique geographic features. Preservation and procurement of open space is sometimes obviated under a program that concentrates primarily upon mandating large-lot subdivisions. The dynamic nature of this phenomenon was highlighted in one case where it was argued that

> the relative advantages of one acre over one-half acre lots are easy to comprehend. Similarly, a two-acre lot has advantages over a one acre lot and three acres may be preferred over two acres or ten acres over three. The greater amount of land, the more room for children, the less congested, the easier to handle water supply and sewage, and the fewer municipal services which must be provided. At some point along the spectrum, however, the size of lots ceases to be a concern requiring public regulation and becomes simply a matter of private preference. The point at which legitimate public interest ceases is not a constant one, but one which varies with the land involved and the circumstances of each case.[40]

The irony is that zoning can be an innovative and novel device to solve the problems of uncontrolled growth, but the inflexibility inherent in these schemes resists further refinements. Subsequently, a static use pattern has emerged with expanding communities enacting rigid controls. As a result, variations from the plan were necessary, provided that the plan's overall character was not jeopardized. One such variation is the special permit.

Special Permit

The separation of use concept legitimized by the *Euclid* decision fostered static and end-state planning. Examining the roles conferred upon the major characters in the land use system, it becomes apparent that the standard enabling acts promulgated what one eminent observer called, "self-administering" rules. The notion was that all future developmental scenarios would be identified and accommodated in a master plan at one shot, with development materializing without the intervention of any further official judgment or discretion.[41] Therefore, to soften the rigidity interposed by this process, relief mechanisms were formulated. The most common of these is the variance, enabling a landowner to apply for a use prohibited under existing zoning ordinances. However, the inability to use this tool on a larger scale—a variance can only be used in the case of a hardship, and only to bring the individual out of the hardship—has fostered the development of the special permit. As a result, municipalities have been afforded some leeway in accommodating activities that posed special control problems.

A special permit would list uses that would be permitted not as a matter of right but rather at the discretion of the local authority and based on articulated criteria and standards. Such an ordinance was enacted in the Village of Sands Point, New York. Under this mechanism land subdivision and residential construction constituted business uses in a residential district and required the granting of a special permit to secure developmental permission. However, the lack of planning documentation behind this provision made it susceptible to a challenge by the Levitt organization in which the court invalidated it due to lack of statutory authority and its arbitrariness.[42] The legal conditions imposed upon the delegating entity seek to protect applicants from unreasonable actions.

In *Lund v. City of Tumwater*[43] the court remarked that the granting of a special use permit specifically authorized in the zoning code was valid because adequate standards had been defined. This decision exemplifies the notion that the granting of a special permit is considered an administrative act and should be based upon clearly articulated objective criteria rather than arbitrary and subjective assumptions.

The concept of special use was considered in *Quigley v. Township of Dexter*[44] in which an ordinance specifying adequacy of public facilities as a prerequisite for a special permit was found to be a reasonable and permissible application of police power. Petaluma, California was confronted with the special permit versus proscribed use doctrine when it initiated its development allotment system. Under the Petaluma system, preliminary municipal approval is required before a builder can apply for traditional plat and building permit permission.[45] Similarly, Ramapo, New York makes building permission contingent upon securing a special use permit.

Experiencing unprecedented and rapid population, housing, service and development growth, Ramapo instituted a point-scaling system, linking development permission to infrastructure capacity. In amending current law, the Ramapo residential development use permit serves as a precursor to other building controls:

> Prior to the issuance of any building permit, special permit of the Board of Appeals, subdivision approval, or site plan approval of the Planning Board for residential development use, a residential developer shall be required to obtain a special permit from the Town Board.[46]

The procedure requires a developer to submit a map showing the location of all his land holdings in the immediate vicinity and the extent of the proposed land development. The applicant indicates the basis of calculating the requisite number of points which would enable the allotment of a special permit. An administrator from the planning board reviews the special permit application, calling upon all relevant sources of information needed to render a decision. Within forty-five days from the plan submission, the town board is notified as to the action taken on the special permit, and in not less than two weeks, the proposal is posted for a public hearing. Within a month after the public review, the board renders its opinion, including the number of units allowable, if indeed a special permit is granted.

But what happens if the municipality articulates its standards, a developer meets them, but the municipality still refuses special permit approval? Though involving a planned development ordinance, a controversy in Middletown Township, Pennsylvania highlights the problem. After granting one medium-sized planned development project, a second developer sought approval of a project. Obviously, the impact of simultaneous PUD projects would create a rate of growth the town did not anticipate. Denied permission, the second developer instituted legal proceedings arguing, on the basis of special exception cases, that once he met the stated requirements of the ordinance, he was entitled to an approval, the burden being on the township to demonstrate some compelling reason why the approval should be denied.[47] Because developers can force municipalities to accommodate all development that satisfies special permit criteria, many municipalities have backed off from adopting special exception ordinances. However, other control devices have been used instead. One is the interim control development ordinance, which we will examine in the following section.

NOTES

1. Village of Euclid v. Ambler Realty Company, 272 U.S. 365 (1926).
2. Zoning development was slow in the United States primarily due to the courts tendency to preserve and protect individual property rights. For further discussion see: Emmet Yorkley, *Zoning Law and Practice,* Third Edition (Charlottesville, Virginia: The Michie Company, 1965), Sections 1-4.
3. American Law Institute, *Model Land Development Code* (Philadelphia: American Law Institute, 1975), Article 1, pp. 2-3.
4. Daniel Mandelker, "The Basic Philosophy of Zoning: Incentives or Restraint," *The New Zonings: Legal, Administrative, and Economic Concepts and Techniques,* edited by Marcus and Groves (New York: Praeger Publishers, 1970), p. 15.
5. Standard State Zoning Enabling Act. Section 26.1.
6. Michael Gleeson et al., "Urban Growth Management Systems," *Planning Advisory Service,* Reports 309 and 310 (Chicago: American Society of Planning Officials, 1975), pp. 23-25.
7. Mang v. County of Santa Barbara, 5 Cal. Rptr. 724 (1960); State ex rel. Randell v. Snohomish 488P. 2d 511 (1971).

8. Norman Williams, *American Land Planning Law,* Vol. III (Chicago: Callaghan and Company, 1975), p. 391.

9. *Ibid.,* p. 392.

10. *Ibid.,* pp. 392-393.

11. *Ibid.*

12. Richard Cutler, "Legal and Illegal Methods for Controlling Community Growth on the Urban Fringe," *Wisconsin Law Review,* 370, 377 (1961), p. 377.

13. 292 P.2d 529 (1956).

14. Southern Burlington County NAACP v. Township of Mount Laurel, 336 A. 2d 713, 719 (1975).

15. 272 U.S. 365, 394 (1926).

16. According to a 1970 Department of Housing and Urban Development survey, 10 percent of the respondents purchased the unit because no other housing was available. However, nearly 40 percent said they bought the mobile dwelling because they preferred this lifestyle. See: U.S., Department of Housing and Urban Development, *Survey of the Owners of New Mobile Homes* (Washington, D.C.: Government Printing Office, 1970).

17. Marvin Moore, "The Mobile Home and the Law," 6 *Akron Law Review,* 1, 9 (1973).

18. California Office of the Legislative Analyst, *The Taxation of Mobile Homes and Mobile Home Parks in California* (Sacramento, California: Office of the Legislative Analyst, 1964), p. 5.

19. Basically, there are four ways of taxing mobile homes: as personal property, as motor vehicles, through periodic fees, or as real property. When taxed as a motor vehicle, collection is facilitated at the expense of not reflecting local assessment ratios due to the state uniform level. When looked upon as personal property this loss of local assessments is overcome; however, this levy is usually ineffectively collected. A periodic fee eliminates the two previous deficiencies but it violates equitable taxation—treating mobile home residents as distinct from other residents. A solution to all these problems is found in taxing the mobile home as real property. See: "Toward an Equitable and Workable Program of Mobile Home Taxation," 71 *Yale Law Journal* 702, 710 (1962).

20. Center for Auto Safety, *Mobile Homes, The Low Cost Housing Hoax* (New York: Grossman Publishers, 1975), pp. 16-19.

21. Sternlieb et al., *Housing Development and Municipal Costs* (New Brunswick, New Jersey: Center for Urban Policy Research, Rutgers University, 1974), pp. 13-30.

22. National cost-revenue analysis, carried on by the Center for Urban Policy Research, has revealed the potential for significant regional variation in the multipliers. However, preliminary analysis has uncovered that persons who live in single-family homes produce more children who attend school than do persons who live in alternative housing. Center for Urban Policy Research, *Regional Variation of Demographic Multipliers,* unpublished, preliminary draft, Center for Urban Policy Research, Rutgers University, New Brunswick, New Jersey, 1975.

23. Miller v. Board of Public Works, 243 P. 381, 386-387 (1925).

24. 263 A. 2d 395 (1970). Apartments were not explicitly prohibited, rather they were allowed via a special permit. Despite this, the court noted that the restrictions on the special permit were too narrow.

25. Township of Williston v. Chesterdale Farms, Inc., 300 A. 2d 107, 121 (1973). Unlike Girsh, where the apartments in question were luxury units, in Chesterdale the court found that not only could the municipality not exclude apartments, solely expensive units were not a viable solution either.
26. 281 A. 2d 401 (1971).
27. Westwood Forest Estates, Inc. v. Village of South Nyack 297 N.Y.S. 2d 129 (1969).
28. 283 A. 2d 353 (1971).
29. Lakeland Bluff, Inc. v. County of Will, 252 N.E. 2d 330 (1969). Edwards v. Township of Montrose, 171 N.W. 2d 555 (1969).
30. *Zoning Digest,* Volume 22, Case 4 (1970), p. 94.
31. National Land and Investment Company v. Easttown Township Board of Adjustment, 215 A. 2d 597, 612 (1965).
32. 89 A. 2d 693 (1952).
33. Charles Haar, "Wayne Township: Zoning For Whom? — In Brief Reply," 67 *Harvard Law Review* 986, 992 (1954).
34. 89 A. 2d 693, 701 (1952).
35. Schere v. Township of Freehold, 292 A. 2d 35 (1972).
36. Steel Hill Development, Inc. v. Town of Sanborton, 496 F. 2d 956 (1972). For an updated analysis of this case, see: Orlando Delogue, *Zoning Digest,* 273 (1975), p. 6.
37. 107 S.E. 2d 390 (1959).
38. *Ibid.,* pp. 394-395.
39. Norman Williams and Edward Wacks, "Segregation of Residential Areas Along Economic Lines: Lionshead Lake Revisited," *Wisconsin Law Review,* 827, 841 (1969).
40. National Land and Investment Company v. Easttown Township Board of Adjustment, 215 A. 2d 597, 608 (1965).
41. Jan Krasnowiecki, "Zoning Litigation and the New Pennsylvania Procedure," 120 *University of Pennsylvania Law Review.* 1029 (1972).
42. Levitt v. Village of Sands Point, 152 N.Y.S. 2d 711 (1956).
43. 472 P. 2d 550 (1970).
44. 204 N.W. 2d 257 (1972).
45. *Residential Development Control System of the City of Petaluma,* Resolution 6113, City of Petaluma, California, 1972.
46. *Special Permit Required For Residential Development Use,* Amendment to Ramapo Town Law, Section 46-13, 1 B, Ramapo, New York.
47. Krasnowiecki, "Zoning Litigation," fn. 63 (p. 1047).

Chapter Four:
Interim Development
Controls

A direct means of retarding growth is to slow or block the development process. Pending the revision of new plans or development regulation, a temporary ordinance can preserve the status quo, denying any other development permission. This is effectuated through: a planning pause; building permit moratoria; and water and sewer moratoria. The rationale is that to preserve the character of the contemplated plan, prevent nonconforming uses, or simply to reassess prevailing controls, temporary "injunctions" against development activity are permissible.

The planning pause allows municipalities, concerned about the direction of their growth, to rethink their goals and objectives without being inundated with requests to build under the present system. Similarly, building, water, and sewer moratoria forestall the issuance of any permits until a new direction of planning has been finalized.

In an effort to preserve the character of the contemplated plan, numerous municipalities have utilized the interim zoning technique. As such, development in accord with only the proposed change is allowed, protecting transitional areas until they are covered by permanent controls. The problem is that the interim regulation is often ill-suited to the objectives it wishes to achieve. Cast as a temporary remedy, it often has little short-term impact yet it may significantly affect the long-term market dynamic. To avoid the temptation to use an interim regulation as a simplistic and eventually adverse planning strategy, a responsible interim policy should be of limited duration and impact, assure fluid transition between the control and the permanent program, and be linked with more expansive management efforts. Specifically, the stop-gap measures enacted as the municipality moves from specific controls to an overall management program should be designed to: preserve the planning process during the implementation stage; prevent creation of nonconforming uses; and promote public debate on the issues involved.[1]

Four basic situations encompass the degree and magnitude of these regulations. Communities adopting a comprehensive plan for the first time need to protect their jurisdiction until the enactment of the plan. Similarly, governmental agencies amending established plans opt for intermediate methods of preserving the existing character of the environment. Moratoria, a form of interim relief, put an abrupt halt on building permits, water and sewer hook-ups, or any other growth generative forms. Lastly, although not as applicable today, interim rules bridge the gap between urban renewal's project delineation and plan adoption.[2] Although it is an old technique, until recently, interim plans were seldom utilized. Now, they have become one of the most frequently used management tools.

Unfortunately, as one commentator has noted, most interim ordinances are nothing more than development moratoria in disguise. The problem is that in many cases the comprehensive planning which is needed to justify the controls has never been formulated. It cannot be overemphasized that interim controls are not a substitute for planning; rather, they are specialized mechanisms geared to achieving limited objectives.[3]

Planning Pause

In the process of developing its new famed sequential and timing plan, Ramapo, New York ordered a freeze on all improvements in areas which were to be subject to zoning change. Within these areas, constituting 75 percent of the town, the issuance of any building permit was prohibited for ninety days. Subsequent amendments extended this ban until the adoption of the master plan. In overriding the plaintiff's contention regarding the constitutionality of this act, the court remarked that the interim plan

is a sensible and practical way to insure that decisions on land usage arrived at on the adoption of the Master Plan but not yet enforceable because the zoning amendments have not been adopted, can be effective provided of course, they be embraced within the amendments.[4]

Ramapo exemplifies the need to keep the planning process intact, in part by preventing uses which do not conform to the proposed future plan and, thus, assuring that the effectiveness of the plan is not destroyed before implementation.

In *Rubin v. McAlevey* the court brought out two additional points regarding the use of the planning pause. The owner (Rubin) had secured a zoning change for his parcel subject to a time limitation, namely that if construction had not started within two years the zoning classification would revert. While numerous motivations can account for this conditioning, a basic justification for the time conscription is to protect the town from the abuse of developers obtaining permits and holding them as a hedge against future zoning changes. The fact that zoning cannot apply retrospectively is well established. However, if an individual owning property has not established a "vested right," the application of a new control on his land is deemed proper.

Providing for public consideration and debate of the plan being proposed should be one of the elements of any interim regulatory strategy. Insuring an adequate time period between the proposal and enactment of a permanent plan is essential to fair and adequate public participation. Such citizen participation was clearly evident in Boca Raton, Florida, where a local group initiated a charter referendum capping total future housing units at 40,000. The enactment of this mandate was supplemented with an interim technique, giving the planning agency adequate time to develop lower density categories, placing the area on a tack of accommodating no more than the 40,000 units. Although prior down-zonings had occurred, the seventeen-month moratorium (spanning November 1972 to April 1974) required that all housing proposals, except single-family and duplex, be subject to review by a moratorium variance advisory board (MVAB—analogous to the Board of Adjustment) before permit and plat approval could be obtained.

Replacing the initial 45-day exaction on multifamily and duplex units, the January 1973 supplement gave the MVAB the responsibility of determining whether the proposed project was in accord with the interim rules established by the city council. Essentially, the planning staff reviewed geographical portions of the city, searching for interim rules consistent with the charter referendum mandate. Upon delineation of these "remedial rezonings" or "cap implementations" the planning board—after fulfilling notice and hearing requirements—would recommend to the city council appropriate actions. Once enacted, the densities established served as parameters for MVAB meetings. Though in many cases the actual densities corresponded to those found in the comprehensive plan, the review in ten zoning districts resulted in an initial density drop of 40 percent, increased to 55 percent and returned to half the intensity previously allowed once permanent controls were established.

Despite the dramatic proportions of this down-zoning, the relative consistency between the imposition and the permanent control enhanced the plan's legitimacy—assuring a more fluid transition between interim and permanent measures. Expanding this criterion, other guidelines for enactment involve the timing of control introduction; control standards; and nonzoning uses.[5]

Timing should reflect the cyclical nature of the permit-filing process. Seasonal fluctuations in many climates necessitate that permit applications be filed in the late winter or early spring. The timing of a stop-gap remedy is directly related to its effectiveness. A permit freeze in the middle of the construction period will have little impact since most development permission will have already been secured. This is not to dismiss the fact that in a period of intensive building a cut-off on permit review may not have some short-term effect. The controversy in Fairfax County, Virginia exemplifies this where at the time of the cut-off date some 60,000 units were in the "pipe-line."

Moratoria

Utilizing its emergency powers, Fairfax's Board of Supervisors instituted an eighteen-month ban (January 1974 to June 1975) on specified building construction. Authorized by an interim development control ordinance, the board froze the construction of subdivisions greater than one lot, townhouses, apartments, and industrial complexes not already approved. Though somewhat less dramatic, the unprecedented levels of growth attained by the county had forced earlier moratoria prohibiting apartment rezonings for the first nine months of 1960.[6] The board did allow construction of projects already approved, public facilities, and single-family homes on properly zoned lots that did not need special permits and that had sewer capability. In accordance with their emergency powers, the supervisors held a public hearing, and on March 4, 1974, formally reaffirmed the intermediate freeze, pending adoption of the plus program. To minimize the harshness of these impositions, subsequent modifications exempted subdivisions of less than 5 acres from the controls, as well as granting immunity to low- and moderate-income housing projects. Additionally, the 180 days construction start specifications on units obtaining development permission were dropped, and all plans received prior to January 7 were to be considered for approval rather than being eliminated from the review process.

In August 1974, the Fairfax County Circuit Court invalidated this ordinance concluding that the presumption of validity attached to the emergency ordinance was overcome by evidence presented and was therefore arbitrary and capricious. Furthermore, the presiding judge held that the board had no express or implied authority to enact either the emergency ordinance or its March update, and the legislation had failed to comply with uniformity requirements.[7] On appeal, the Virginia Supreme Court agreed with the lower court's ruling holding that the Fairfax County Board of Supervisors had no express or implied authority to enact ordinances imposing moratorium on the filing of site plans and preliminary subdivision plots:

> There is no statutory authority for the enactment of an interim development ordinance which suspends the submission of site plans for a specified period of time.[8]

In assessing the usefulness of an interim development strategy as a step toward more comprehensive growth management, it seems that the interim technique is being used for something it cannot achieve. Interim ordinances can provide for a pause in the planning process; however, they cannot be effectively used to stop development, even in the short-run, if there is already mounting development pressure. Fairfax is a case in point. At its cut-off date, there were still 60,000 units exempted from the moratoria, generating enough growth not to substantially disturb the short-range market. However, this initial restraining effect would substantially alter the decentenial picture (1974-1984), potentially resulting in a two-fifths drop in the rate of new homes built.[9] While obviously a growth-limiting device, the interim technique is a short-range instrument, designed to handle immediate problems but not to adversely affect long-term market dynamics. Yet, due to the 60,000 potential units not exempted by the moratorium, Fairfax's interim remedy did little to arrest short-term development. A recent study conducted for the U.S. Department of Housing and Urban Development concluded that in the Washington Metropolitan Area "the (sewer) moratoria did not appear to slow down either construction permits or starts."[10] Citing Montgomery County, Maryland as a prime example, the study revealed that although the area had been encumbered with various moratoria since 1970, the county in 1972 experienced a 24,000 population increase—the largest in its history.

In May of 1970 a moratorium imposed by the Maryland Department of Health placed a sewer ban in the Anacostia and Cabin John watersheds in Montgomery County.[11] This action, premised on impending capacity shortages and inadequate trunkline facilities, caused a run on permits in nondeveloped watershed areas, as well as stimulating development in the sewered portions of the interstices. A following 1972 action by the Washington Suburban Sanitary Commission halted authorization on new sewer trunkline construction in the whole county, pending a study of sewer capacity. This carried over to the building trades in that no building permits were granted without prior approval of sewer construction. Despite an additional freeze of proposed subdivisions in areas conflicting with the pending growth plan, a 1973 reassessment of the interim strategy reported that

> the results (of the moratoria) have been disappointing. The increase in sewage flows has not tapered off. The residential construction rate has actually increased. Despite the fact that authorizations for sewer extensions

have virtually ceased, there is no evidence that the moratorium is having the desired effect of either limiting or staging flows. . . One effect appears to be a stimulation of construction activity, as measured through a stimulation of infilling development on vacant ground where only a sewer connection and no authorization is needed.[12]

Completing the assessment of their measures, the report by the executive office of the county concluded that "the end result is that both water quality and socio-economic problems have gotten worse."[13]

While the prospect of arresting short-term problems via a moratorium is uncertain, in response to insufficient trunk capacity, system overflows, or inadequate treatment facilities, municipalities have used moratoria to freeze new sewer authorizations and connections, ban the issuance of new building permits, and restrict subdivision or rezoning requests.

The high costs of adequate sewage treatment coupled with an initial impoundment of federal water pollution control aid have contributed to the popularity of imposing a moratorium on new sewer facilities. Brooklyn Park, Minnesota imposed such a moratorium. Fearful that the additional sanitary capacity created by the construction of a trunkline would be fully utilized before new sewer extensions were reviewed, Brooklyn Park initiated a five-month ban on requests for special permits or for subdivision approval, pending a reappraisal of sanitary sewer capacity. Similarly, Livermore, California residents drafted an ordinance calling for a freeze on building permits until the problems of water and sewage were satisfactorily addressed. On December 29, 1972 this ordinance was invalidated as being overbroad, violating due process, and without character or statutory authority.[14] Despite this ruling, other repetitive measures have been promulgated along the lines of:

1. The failure to achieve accepted levels of organic, sediment and nutrient removal;
2. Major leaks in the network which transmit wastes to the treatment facilities;
3. The use of the same sewer network to carry sanitary, industrial and storm water waster to treatment facilities; and
4. The presence or threat of major developments which rely on septic tanks.[15]

Unfortunately, while insufficient sewer capacity is reasonable justification to freeze development, such insufficiency is not common in the 1970s. Central cities have long grappled with the first three issues: "Given the existence of sewer system problems long before 1970, it follows that the moratorium device has been developed as a treatment for problems which are much larger than site specific environmental degradation."[16]

One of these larger problems involves the freezing of the issuance of building permits in conjunction with a sewer moratorium.

Such a constraint was utilized in New Castle, New York in 1956. An amendment to the local law provided that no more than 112 annual residential building permits be issued for any land deemed special residence. The declaration—which placed practically all residential land in this special category—further specified that the permits be allocated one quarter for each June 1st and September 1st quarter, with 15 percent allotted to the quarter beginning December 1st and the remaining proportions credited to the quarter beginning March 1st. In declaring this quota unconstitutional the court noted that it was not only outside the scope of the municipal power but it simultaneously comprised a taking of property without just compensation.[17] A parallel to this ruling was the court's decree in *U.S. Home and Development Corporation v. LaMura.*[18] A slate of town officials elected on a nongrowth platform passed an amendment to the building code of the Town of Marlboro, New Jersey. The amendment specified the number of permits made available to a developer during various construction stages. Accordingly, the initial ten allowable permits could be added to upon the completion of the foundations for the initial ten. Ten more permits were dispensed when the first ten buildings were framed and the second ten were at the foundation-completion stage. This process repeated itself in series of tens through a four-step construction cycle, covering forty dwellings at a time. In annulling this effort, the court found it to be an arbitrary and unreasonable exercise of the police power.

Avoiding quantitative limitations, Dade County, Florida put together an interim plan which included a building freeze. Fragmentary development patterns, based on rezoning actions, were threatening to encroach significant ecosytems; the possibility of this event prompted Key Biscayne residents to push for a construction ban. The request was rejected twice, then made some headway in 1971, only to fail to generate enough support from the county commissioners. However, the requisite 10 percent resident voter signatures were secured and a referendum was forced. The ratification of this March 1972 measure mandated establishment of building moratoria parameters on unincorporated areas. A complementary action in zoning changes was instituted by the end of 1972, with a review procedure facilitating the renewed 1973 moratoria measure.

Pending adoption of the revised comprehensive plan, the Dade County commissioners determine the nature and the extent of a moratorium area based on the planning department's recommendations. A time limit is then placed on the stop-gap measure, enabling an assessment of the area. After the assessment and the public hearing, the commissioners decide which course of action to pursue. If the current zoning is deemed suitable, the imposition is lifted. If revised specifications are charted, these regulations continue until other related county departments are apprised of such a plan and can amend their plans accordingly. While the majority of programs emanate from the local level, in one case the federal government moved to enjoin Douglas County, Nevada from issuing building permits for

> the construction of any new buildings, residences and facilities in the areas in Douglas County, Nevada ... until facilities for the treatment and exploration of waste and sewage from the Lake Tahoe Basin have been completed and placed in operation.[19]

In summary, municipalities attempting to devise a management strategy can employ the interim technique to hold development until the comprehensive plan is completed and approved. However, interim controls cannot substitute for a comprehensive program. In a study sponsored by the American Society of Planning Officials, David Heeter concluded that interim programs were frequently ill-suited to the objectives which they sought to achieve.[20] In a larger context, stop-gap measures represent a simplistic solution to a complex problem. Most interim actions are initiated in response to specific and immediate problems: "The evidence is not compelling that governmental bodies responsible have considered the bulk of the relevant issues—or indeed are taking steps to do so now that the impacts are being felt."[21]

While interim arrangements can protect the integrity of the planning process during transition, their serious drawbacks—possibly producing imbalances in housing production, discriminating against low- and moderate-housing development, creating hardships for those who don't have the staying power to last out a moratorium, and perpetuating sprawl in nondeveloped jurisdictions—necessitate extreme caution before interim development controls are adopted.

NOTES

1. Robert Freilich, "Interim Development Controls: Essential Tools For Implementing Flexible Planning and Zoning," 49 *Journal of Urban Law*, 65 (1971).
2. David Heeter, "Interim Zoning Ordinances," *Planning Advisory Service*, Report Number 242 (Chicago: American Society of Planning Officials, 1969), pp. 7-9.
3. *Ibid.*, p. 30.
4. 282 N.Y.S. 2d 564 and 568 (1967).
5. Freilich, "Interim Development," pp. 93-95.
6. Terry Peters, *The Politics and Administration of Land Use Control* (Lexington, Massachusetts: Lexington Books, 1974), p. 27.
7. Board of Supervisors of Fairfax County v Horne 215 S.E. 2d 453, 455 (1975).
8. *Ibid.*, p. 457.
9. Mason Hirst, Inc., *Total Future Homebuilding in Fairfax County: 1974-1984, Given Current Sewer Policies* (Annandale, Virginia: Mason Hirst, Inc., 1974), p. 1.

10. Rivkin-Carson, Inc., *The Sewer Moratorium as a Technique of Growth Control and Eivironmental Protection,* Number PB-230 293 (Springfield, Virginia: National Technical Information Service, 1973), p. 22.
11. Smoke Rise, Inc. v. Washington Suburban Sanitary Commission, U.S. District Court for Maryland, August 8, 1975, upheld this moratorium.
12. Office of the County Executive, *Memorandum to the County Council on Sewer Authorizations* (Montgomery County, Maryland: Office of County Executive), p. I-1.
13. *Ibid.,* p. IV-2.
14. Associated Home Builders of Greater East Bay, Inc. v. City of Livermore, Memorandum Decision Number 425754, December 29, 1972.
15. Michael Greenberg, "A Commentary on the Sewer Moratorium as a Piecemeal Remedy for Controlling Development," *Growth Controls,* edited by James Hughes (New Brunswick, New Jersey: Center for Urban Policy Research, Rutgers University, 1974), p. 190.
16. *Ibid.*
17. Albrecht Realty Company, Inc. v. Town of New Castle, 167 N.Y.S. 2d 843 (1957).
18. 214 A. 2d 538 (1965).
19. Rivkin-Carson, *Sewer Moratorium,* p. 21.
20. Heeter, "Interim Zoning," p. 7.
21. Rivkin-Carson, *Sewer Moratorium,* p. 27.

Chapter Five:
Division of Land

Next to zoning, division of land is the second most common management device. This technique indirectly controls growth through regulating the location, pace, and quality of land development. As such, many second generation public facility plans evolved from land division techniques. Regulations over land division are aimed at facilitating sound and orderly growth in accordance with the municipal plan. Basically four elements help achieve this end: subdivision regulations; annexation policies; official map; and exactions.

Broader in scope than zoning, subdivision regulations establish conditions which must be complied with prior to plan approval. This assures adequacy of the necessary supportive services before development permission can be granted. An annexation policy prevents discordant development by reviewing the proposed annexation in terms of its consistency with the overall growth management strategy. Annexation is conditioned upon the jurisdiction's service capacity; if such capacity is inadequate to handle increased service, annexation does not take place.

Though another indirect management method, the official map differs slightly from land division controls in that it specifies contemplated areas of public works—roads, sewer, etc. Development inconsistent with that of already developed areas is then prohibited. Unlike subdivision, annexation, and official map policies on the adequacy of public facilities, exactions concern themselves with the equalization of service demand generated. The dedication of money, land, or improvements is a prerequisite to plat approval. However, caution needs to be exercised so that all the burden to provide the necessary services is not thrown on the developer. Therefore, to be effective exactions must: provide for an equal level of municipal infrastructure responsibility; be backed with municipal financial commitment to help provide the necessary services; and be integrated with other management techniques.

Subdivision Control

The authorization of zoning legitimized separate land classiciation require-ments. While zoning regulations have been expanded as previously described, the Standard Zoning Enabling Act (SZEA) overlooked the broader planning functions needed to support the segregation of land uses. Though Section 3 of the SZEA deemed that regulations be made "in accordance with a comprehensive plan," the act does not specify how to formulate such a plan. Additionally, regulations to guide the planning of streets, platting of lands, and provision of sufficient public facilities are conspicuously lacking.[1] To achieve these ends, subdivision regulations were authorized by the Standard City Planning Enabling Act (SPEA). Providing broader powers than zoning, the SPEA enabled its administrators to "agree with the applicant upon use, height, area or bulk requirements or restrictions governing buildings and premises within the subdivision."[2] Given the magnitude of growth municipalities have experienced and the increasing awareness, on the part of both the judiciary and the planner, of the need to rationally assimilate this expansion, subdivision regulations have advanced to the point at which construction can be conditioned to off-site, as well as on-site characteristics. Such considerations may include requirements that:

— Adequate water supply will be provided for the residents of the subdivision.
— The land used will not induce flooding, create water pollution or adversely impact shorelands or wetlands regions.
— Off-site roads leading to the subdivision are adequate to handle the volume of traffic generated.[3]

The subdivision process involves the division, possibly followed by the sale, of a site into smaller parcels. While isolated instances of this phenomenon are not threatening, large-scale replication — such as that which has occurred in connection with post-World War II suburbanization — establishes a definite pattern of community growth. In this context, control over the nature and extent of subdivision activity should be integrated within a management program.

In its most generic form, subdivision requirements relate to the provision or installation of internal, site-specific improvements. Road widths, setbacks, sewer outlets and drainage locations are systematically delineated. Broader applications can also be exercised on the basis of the subdivision plan's relationship to the environment. A municipality charting a growth framework can look to the subdivision ordinance as a means of integrating future development with the provision of adequate services or reducing present or anticipated adverse impacts. Besides conditioning development, subdivision ordinances can provide for outright prohibition if the project proposed is not in accord with the management plan or if substantial physical or environmental damages would ensue. However, there is a tenuous line between legitimate public concerns and blatant parochialism.

Evidence of this latter was brought forth in an early Connecticut case. As detailed in a following section, a developer in the Town of Milford advanced a subdivision plan consistent with the town's ordinance. However, the proposed development was disapproved on grounds that Milford would be financially unable to provide school facilities for the project's anticipated student population. Ensuing litigation over the lack of authorized and adequate standards rendered the town's decision invalid.[4]

Notwithstanding the validity of judicially imposed limits, the growing realization is that it is unfair to impose the entire servicing cost of a new development on the municipality. This realization has led to the prescription of exactions in the form of land or money dedications by the developer to the municipality. Supplementing this measure, officially mapping future infrastructure extensions, within a reasonable time period, can have a legally binding effect on those proposing development. In this regard, annexation policies, in the form of preventing discontinuous development in contiguous areas or prohibiting boundary extension altogether, have also been helpful.

In the case of linking subdivision and annexation policies, one observer has noted that in expanding cities where annexation is imminent, extraterritorial subdivision has often been upheld, enabling the applicant seeking annexation to forestall any future problems.[5] In the following section, annexation and other land division options will be examined in a growth management context.

Annexation

A municipality's geographic limits determine not only its population and territoriality limitations but also the extent of its available service resources. Thus, the judicial absorption of one area by another can have a beneficial effect on the relationship between territory and resources. Annexation can be justified as a means to prevent discordant development, with appropriate restrictions then placed on the acquired land. Though jurisdiction variations exist, many localities are empowered to reject annexation on the basis of its potentially adverse impact. In accordance with statutory requirements, the appropriate decision-making agency can then evaluate the proposed annexation in terms of its consistency with the growth control scheme. For example, in the process of developing its 500-building permit restriction, Petaluma, California designated an urban extension line indicating the ultimate growth boundary line for twenty years. Annexation or extension of facilities to areas beyond this line was disallowed.

Another California community, Livermore, established an annexation standard as part of an overall growth control plan. The Livermore Planning Commission studies areas to be annexed and provides information pertaining to allowable uses. Residents or developers in the annexed area are then informed of the Livermore growth design and the restrictions pertaining to that design prior to annexation.

Broadening this function, Minnesota has established a municipal commission which is empowered to hold land for future annexation until such a time as the area to be annexed has the capacity to furnish urban services. Similarly, the cooperative planning occurring between Marion County and Salem, Oregon exemplify a process in which requests for subdivision, rezoning, or permits—necessitating water and sewer hook-ups—in outlying areas are scrutinized by a boundary commission. Upon finding that the request is consistent with the Salem growth plan, the area is then annexed and can then apply for specific building or service permits.

While additional applications of the annexation process exist, it is important to note that it is but one land division technique designed to facilitate the implementation of growth plans. Its effectiveness is strengthened when aligned with other mechanisms, one of which is the official map.

Official Map

In general, the official map designates street placement and public improvement action, with particular emphasis on the location and extent of these activities. As such, it can be a valuable tool in guiding the course of community expansion. Basically, the map has four important functions:

— Inventory: the map shows not only the precise location of future improvements, but also the exact boundaries of the public right of way, the exact legal grades, and so forth,
— Future Location: the map designates proposed future streets and parks, not yet publicly acquired.
— Prohibition against building: once the land has been placed on the official

map, the ordinance prohibits any further construction on land shown in the bed of future streets.

Modification: if land as it has been publicly designated cannot provide a reasonable return to the landowner, then a local administrative agency is authorized to minimize the adverse impact on the landowner.[6]

The purpose of these delineations is to promote orderly city growth and development, eliminating the haphazard construction of buildings and service facilities which would be inconsistent with future street networks. As with subdivision regulations, the power and effectiveness of official maps has increased. Broadening the street specification authority, localities can now chart potential parks, playgrounds, drainage areas and sites for other public improvements. While some judicial circumspection is imposed on the latter, it can become a powerful tool in that public sewer and water facilities are often installed in the bed of a charted road. Utility extension regulations can also guard against premature land conversion. The map puts the developer on notice as to the nature and extent of the future improvements, while simultaneously providing a commitment as to the facilities the community intends to provide.

Though somewhat more integrated and comprehensive in scope, Ramapo's timing and sequential controls program has the same effect. Delineations of future infrastructure capabilities are made with development conditioned on the existence of such services. Proposals inconsistent with charted extensions are denied.

While the process of defining future improvements is similar to master planning, the novelty surrounding the official map is its legally binding nature. It serves as a blueprint for the comprehensive plan. For example, under the authority of the official map, a municipality can forbid the issuance of a building permit within the boundaries of a proposed way. Municipal utility extension can be denied in streets which do not appear on the map. The map is a projection of future development, reinforced and implemented by legal limits. Accordingly:

if the path of future highways is determined and municipal facilities are required to follow mapped streets, the general control over urban form is established, since subdivision plats not in accords with the official map are not accepted.[7]

Validation of this action comes under the realm of the police power; reasonableness is determined on the basis of the temporary nature of the restriction. The map allows for the title and possession of a particular area to remain with the owner, with just compensation provided only when and if the area is publicly appropriated. The frequently scattered location of these areas has been found to represent a considerable barrier to officials attempting to link roads around them. This is not to say that a government agency either can or should depress an individual's land value, reducing the basis of just compensation, in order to prevent the owner from building on the areas which the city proposes to acquire at some future date. Such a position was averred in *Headly v. Rochester,*[8] in which the court legitimized the city's position, viewing the map law as a compromise between permitting uncontrolled development and condemnation. However, unconditional use of this tactic has not been forthcoming. A decision in favor of modification was rendered in *Lomarch Corp. v. Mayor of Englewood.*[9] The 1953 New Jersey Official Map and Building Permit Act authorized the municipality to reserve, for one year, the right to acquire the officially mapped portions of the Lomarch Corporation's property after the final plat approval. The court noted that the reservation constituted an option of purchase and therefore a taking of an interest in land. Similarly, a Pennsylvania statute empowering a locality to designate parks via official mapping, and then reserve the right to acquire the parcels for up to three years, was found to be *ultra vires* and constituted a taking without compensation.[10] Case law has established a number of criteria to indicate the appropriateness of reserving land on the basis of official maps:

— How much of the lot is affected by the restoration?
— Is the remainder of the unreserved portion useable for some appropriate use in view of the surrounding land use pattern?
— How long are the restrictions to last?[11]

In addition to legal questions, the official map in a growth plan context poses certain difficulties which impinge upon its large-scale effectiveness. The first of these concerns the importance of precise drafting of the areas to be designated. Delineating building lines on accurate base maps is crucial to the effectiveness of the map. Other technical considerations involve the types of improvements to be designated (should minor streets be mapped?) and the need to keep the maps current. In a broader context, a municipality attempting to devise a growth plan cannot rely on the official map alone. The purpose of the map is to keep areas free from impediments to future use, rather than to prhoibit all uses. Complete prohibition constitutes a taking, necessitating compensation. Aside from this issue, the preparation and proper execution of a mapping strategy involves substantial costs in surveying and drafting. Caution needs to be exercised so that the ultimate design is compatible with the natural features and capacity of the land.

The official map can be looked upon as a useful but limited tool. This characteristic of the official map became evident in the Dade County Metropolitan Guide. Beset with increased growth and fragmented development, the county revised its 1965 land use plan in order to emphasize coordinated and harmonious development. In doing so, it identified and reserved the locations of public facilities. The planning board went on to note that "by knowing which parcels of land are going to be used for public purposes, private landowners are able to plan their developments in a manner physically and functionally consistent with the government's plan for acquiring rights-of-way for highways and transit."[12] However, the complexity of the Date situation, coupled with the previously discussed official map limitations, necessitates the introduction of complementary measures; one such is the exaction.

Exactions

Growth regulating measures have been spurred by the continual influx of residents into new territories, spiraling service costs and taxes, loss of open space, and a general deterioration in the quality of life. Municipal officials are faced with the dilemma of how to bridge the gap between the costs of providing adequate capital facilities and services without imposing extraordinary revenue burdens on the established property owners in the community. Expanding a technique used fifty years ago, subdivision ordinances are mandating dedication of land or fees in lieu thereof to lessen the adversity of the new development. These requirements can be integrated within a growth management plan by securing adequate vestiges of open space, imposing service costs upon the new residents, and requiring the provision of adequate capital facilities both on- and off-site. Specifically, conditions municipalities may require prior to plat approval include: land dedication or reservation; monetary fees; completion of specific improvements; and impact taxes.[13]

Land dedication or reservation addresses the setting aside of parkland or other support facilities including sewer, school sites, and streets. The rationale is to equalize the service generated by the new housing, even if some requirements extend off-site. The monetary variation enables a cash payment to the municipality to purchase a school or park site instead of the developer setting a parcel aside. The reason is that the developing site may be too small for a piece to be donated, or its location may be ill-suited for the required public use. The third exaction conditions project acceptance to the furnishing of certain items deemed necessary to the welfare of the prospective inhabitants and the community at large. Finally, impact taxes are a means of securing an amount of money from a restricted group of property owners in order to defray the cost of a particular improvement or service.

Mary Brooks has identified two principal means for arriving at the extent of the dedication: a fixed percentage as a function of the subdivision's total land area, and a density formula, specifying a given amount of land per unit.[14] The variability of the fixed percentage multiplier is virtually limitless, within the reasonableness of the law, but tends toward the 5-20 percent range. Density formulas may be constructed on the basis of a required portion per intensity of parcel use or by extricating dedicated amounts as a function of the number of units in the proposal. The amount of money required in place of property acquisition can be calculated upon the assessed or fair market value of the land, a fixed amount per unit, or by a variable amount of the fair market value as a function of the intensity of the subdivision.[15] Boulder, Colorado utilizes the first two methods in its growth strategy. Along with its open space acquisition program, the city, in 1967, embarked on a "pay as you go program." Under this policy, $850 is collected from the developer of new construction if the construction is linked to the water system; there is a similar $450 charge for a sewer hook-up. Augmenting this, a park fee of $150 per single unit ($25 less per multiple family unit) is imposed on the developer for acquisition and development of the neighborhood. This latter stipulation highlights one of the general litigation guidelines: that there must be a reasonable relationship between the financial requirement demanded from the developers or residents of the subdivision and the benefit accruing to them. This principle was upheld in *Pioneer Trust and Savings v. Village of Mount Prospect*[16] in which the court stipulated that exactions imposed must be specifically attributable to the subdivision's activity and not to the general public. However, according to Heyman and Gilhool, the traditional view is that an exaction is permissible as long as there is some relationship between the imposition and the revenues generated by the development.[17]

Returning to Boulder's growth control strategy, the other technique used was the percentage allocation formula, allowing the municipality to collect 0.5 to 1 percent of a new commercial or industrial building's cost for the park fee kitty. A supplementary program exempts the charges levied on low- and moderate-income housing upon finding that the costs act as a deterrent to construction.

Dade County, Florida's development guide is less specific. However, it does mention that even if slack infrastructure capacity exists, developer's services could be paid in cash: "The existence of services does not lessen the obligation of the developer to pay for its capital service costs, it merely changes the method of meeting this obligation."[18] This position seems to run contrary to another legal test of an exaction's propriety, namely the reasonableness of the relationship between the requirement and the need for the development.[19]

Loudoun County, Virginia's requirements hinge upon the location of the development. If the subdivision ordinance specified a park, school or other public facility on the developer's parcel, the planning commission may require a dedication. If the project is in accord with the plan, but the zoning is inconsistent, Article 12 of the Loudoun County Zoning Ordinance gives the developer the option to compensate the county for increased capital costs associated with the project or to make the improvements himself, transferring them to the appropriate agency after completion. This latter approach is similar to that of Ramapo, New York. As one way out from a potential eighteen-year restraint on land, the developer can advance the building date through providing the requisite facilities himself. Typically, the "buy-out" consists of drainage improvements, improved roads, or additional recreational facilities. However, the enormous cost of constructing a sewer system or building a fire station has virtually eliminated these options.[20]

The critical water shortage in Pinellas County, Florida resulted in county officials requiring that the water department approve the right to operate the on-site well water source until the department had the capacity to link the parcel into the county's system. Without such authorization, the Pinellas County Health Department would not approve any building permit application.

In assessing the various dedication methods, the fixed percentage formula is primarily attractive because of its simplicity. Once the multiplier is specified it is merely applied to the size of the subdivision in order to determine the extent of the exaction. However, the advantage in the ease of application is qualified by the inability of the fixed percentage formula to account for intensity of use. While a 100-acre, single-family development would generate different service demands than the same parcel with apartments, the exactions, figured by fixed percentage formulas, would be equal due to the common 100-acre basis. A density scale establishes a set relationship between the project's use and the size of the dedication; however, it enables the single-family units to escape much of the exaction burden, perpetuating low-density development. A flat fee per unit hits hardest at those with lower incomes while a sliding or progressive fee structure imposes increased costs on those at the other end of the income spectrum.

A popular argument against in-lieu payments is that they increase the already high cost of housing, effectively minimizing the number of individuals who can compete in the market. In recognition of this increased burden upon low- and moderate-income families, some localities have required the developer to set aside a fixed proportion of units to meet low-income housing needs. In *Board of Supervisors of Fairfax County v. DeGroff Enterprises*[21] the validity of Fairfax County Zoning Amendment 156 was tested. This measure stipulated that developers of fifty or more units in certain zoning districts were to commit 15 percent of the units to low- and moderate-income levels (consistent with HUD guidelines) prior to rezoning or site plan approval. Despite the uncontroverted need for over 10,000 of these units in the Fairfax area, the court found the action *ultra vires* and an attempt to control the compensation for the use of land and improvements therein.[22] Undeterred by invalidation in its neighboring state, Montgomery County, Maryland passed similar legislation in 1973. The resolution mandates that all applicants who apply for a building permit and want to use the existing sewer facilities must submit a written agreement to the County's Department of Environmental Protection that not less than 15 percent of any development of fifty or more dwelling units are moderately priced. In the "town sector and planned neighborhood zones" the requirement is 20 percent.[23]

Boulder, Colorado uses the same 15 percent level as an annexation or utility extension condition.

Exactions can play a useful role in establishing a level of balance between users and services as well as securing open space and other public facility sites. However, it is crucial to ascertain the extent to which newcomers do actually increase the burden on existing residents. Inflation, changes in the proportion of various age groups in the population, and prior service deficiencies are other variables impacting the municipal fisc. Nevertheless, potential residents should not have to subsidize current inhabitants for these inadequacies; the municipality must assume some responsibility. Unfortunately, what is happening now is that the rules are getting switched on the developer in the middle of the game. Traditionally the bill for increased service costs was financed under municipal indebtedness. Bonds would be floated. Now, the burden is on the developer to pay these costs, and since these payments come up front, exaction funds are financed from the construction loan at a high interest rate (10-12 percent). This is considerably higher than what the municipality could float a bond at (6-8 percent). There are other intervening techniques that can also provide the basic capital requirements to sustain growth and development—for example, special districting, incorporation, or formation of private utility companies.[24]

If the exaction route is still preferable, a ceiling or an upper limit should be attached to it. Otherwise its utility can be subverted, turning it into an exclusionary measure. Boulder's exemption of low- and moderate-income housing from link-up charges is commendable. Setting aside units for lower income residents addresses the exclusionary gap, but prescribing a set quota is not the only possible answer. Though units have not been built, Petaluma's rewarding builders extra "development points" for provision of some lower cost housing is another alternative. This approach could have been instituted in Ramapo to reduce exclusionary effects.[25]

An ironic twist of fates can occur if the municipality seeks to absolve itself from any financial or social responsibility. As Norman Williams perceptively pointed out, "subdivision control as now administered tends to be antiecological, for the municipal determination to avoid any subsequent cost for further improvements leads to decisions for more and more paving and disturbance of the natural landscape."[26]

Over the past few years, there has been a movement to more expansive growth management programs—programs which establish a municipal fiscal and social commitment to provide the requisite facilities for a growing population. These "second generation" techniques address the shortcomings of zoning and subdivision. They integrate and broaden traditional methodologies with the objective of regulating land conversion and insuring some performance level in regard to infrastructure provision. These methods will be explored in the following section.

NOTES

1. For a more refined treatment of this issue, see: Jan Krasnowiecki, "Zoning Litigation and the New Pennsylvania Procedure," 120 *University of Pennsylvania Law Review* 1028 (1972).
2. U.S. Department of Commerce, *A Standard City Planning Enabling Act,* Section 15 (Washington, D.C.: Government Printing Office, 1928).
3. Robert Freilich and John Ragsdale, Jr., "Timing and Sequential Controls—The Essential Basis for Effective Regional Planning: An Analysis of New Directions for Land Use Control in the Mineapolis-St. Paul Metropolitan Region," 58 *Minnesota Law Review* 1009 (1974).
4. Beach v. Planning and Zoning Commission of the Town of Milford, 103 A. 2d 814 (1954).
5. Norman Williams, *American Land Planning Law,* Vol. 5 (Chicago: Callaghan and Company, 1975), p. 276.
6. *Ibid.,* p. 257.
7. Freilich and Ragsdale, "Timing," p. 1062.
8. 5 N.E. 2d 198 (1936).
9. 237 A. 2d 881 (1968).
10. Miller v. Beaver Falls, 82A. 2d 34 (1951).
11. Williams, *American Land,* p. 269.
12. Dade County Planning Department, *Comprehensive Development Master Plan, Part 3, Metropolitan Development Guide For Metropolitan Dade County, Florida* (Dade County, Florida: Dade County Planning Department, 1974), p. 232.
13. "Allocating the Burden of Increased Community Costs Caused by New Development," 1967 *University of Illinois Law Forum* 318 (1967).
14. Mary Brooks, "Mandatory Dedication of Land or Fees in Lieu of Land for Parks and Schools," *Planning Advisory Service* (Chicago: American Society of Planning Officials, 1971), Report Number 266, p. 10.
15. *Ibid.,* pp. 13-14.
16. 176 N.E. 2d 79 (1961).
17. Ira Heyman and Thomas Gilhool, "The Constitutionality of Imposing Increased Community Costs on New Subdivision Residents Through Subdivision Exactions," 73 *Yale Law Journal* 1119, 1137 (1964).
18. Dade County Planning Department, p. 223.
19. Brooks, "Mandatory Dedication," p. 7.
20. Manuel Emanuel, "Ramapo's Managed Growth Program: A Close Look at Ramapo After Five Years," *Planners Notebook,* 4/5 (Washington, D.C.: American Institute of Planners, 1974), p. 8.
21. 198 S.E. 2d 600 (1973).
22. *Ibid.,* p. 602.
23. The Potomac Institute Inc., *Summary of Moderately Priced Dwelling Unit Regilations Adopted by the Montgomery County Council,* Memorandum 73-11 (Washington, D.C.: The Potomac Institute, Inc., 1973).
24. James Mitchell, "Special Districting in Financing and Facilitating Urban Growth," 5 *The Urban Lawyer* 185 (1973).
25. Herbert Franklin, *Controlling Growth—But For Whom?* (Washington, D.C.: The Potomic Institute, Inc., 1974).
26. Williams, *American Land,* p. 290.

Section II
Second Generation Techniques

Section II
Second Generation Techniques

Since the early 1920, planners have set about to influence the direction and magnitude of community growth. Zoning provisions enabled the dissection of a jurisdiction into classifications encompassing a variety of uses. Subdivision regulations were created and gave the planner control over on-site specifications. Building codes reinforced this process by enabling municipal officials to set adequacy standards for construction. Though these techniques have been the major components of the land use system throughout the twentieth century, they have become increasingly sophisticated and significant strategies. While initially quite innovative, the narrow scope of building codes eventually contributed to static, end-state planning. Accordingly, the Standard State Zoning Enabling Act and Standard City Planning Enabling Act established a divisive approach to development control: use, bulk, height, and spacing requirements were spelled out under the SZEA with the distribution of buildings and site improvements singled out for the SPEA. Thus, "a cleavage occurred at the heart of the land use control system: the control of use, bulk, height, and spacing of buildings (zoning) was separated from subdivision or site planning control."[1] Unfortunately, the majority of development plans involve both sets of controls, yet each is administered separately.

The notion at the beginning of the century was that the planner could sit down and, at one shot, determine all future needs, accommodating them in a master plan. Naturally deviations would arise; however the initial planning options to change this system were narrowly constructed. When examining the three powers the Standard State Zoning Enabling Act gave to the administrative agency, only the special exception suggests that the local legislative body might establish some general standards short of self-administering rules, allowing the board discretion to interpret and apply them in each particular case.

It is unrealistic to think that planners would have the foresight to determine future needs once and for all, but even if they did, traditional land use controls have absolutely no provisions for timing. The sequence and location of development was left to market forces. The nonsense of this approach is now apparent. Municipalities often did not have the physical, social, or fiscal capability to expand commensurate with population and service demands. In addition, the local legislative body would want to be able to scrutinize any proposed development. Accordingly:

> At the metropolitan scale, the present techniques of development guidance have not effectively controlled the time and location of development. Under traditional zoning, jurisdictions are theoretically called upon to determine in advance the sites needed for various types of development. . . . In doing so they have continued to rely on techniques which were never designed as timing devices and which do not function well in controlling timing. The attempt to use large lot zoning, for example, to control timing has all too often resulted in scattered development on large lots, prematurely establishing the character of much later development—the very effect sought to be avoided. New types of controls are needed if the basic metropolitan scale problems are to be solved.[2]

Faced with these limitations, local officials set zoning controls at a level just below the threshold at which development could actually occur. Consequently, major land use determinations are not "in accordance with a comprehensive plan"; rather they are the byproducts of rezoning. As dismaying as this might seem to those who are trained to be comprehensive, how else can the disparity between the plan and actual development be explained? "Thus, in the name of generality based on an abhorrence of individualized treatment, we permit local governments to operate a *discriminatory quota system* without requiring that they state the principles upon which it is based."[3] (Emphasis added.)

Because of these deficiencies, many communities have enacted growth management systems in order to control and time development on the basis of a well articulated plan. Permission to develop is then contingent upon the growth plan and its attendant regulations. Though guiding, inducing, or limiting growth is not a new phenomenon, what is novel about these second generation management techniques is that they integrate individual development provisions into a package of controls. Four "advanced" second generation techniques have been proposed: cap rates, annual permit limitations, adequate facility provisions, and the one to which we now turn, urban service boundaries.

NOTES

1. Jan Z. Krasnowiecki, "Zoning Litigation and the New Pennsylvania Procedures," 120 *University of Pennsylvania Law Review,* 1029, (1972).
2. Clyn Smith III, "Comments: Easements to Preserve Open Space Land," I, *Ecology Law Quarterly,* 728, (1971).
3. *Supra* 1, p. 1034.

Chapter Six:
Urban Service Areas

Basically, the designation of urban service areas identifies where growth should occur, and with a cordon or boundary line, establishes the geographical extent to which development is permissible. It is an indirect means of controlling growth in that it channels development rather than limits it.

Defining the boundary is critical. It should be based upon a realistic assessment of existing and projected demographic forces. Some lines are defined as areas in which service will be provided; others show capital improvement plans with a resulting service boundary. In articulating these limits, caution needs to be exercised so that land supply is not too severely constricted; otherwise the plan could trigger artificially inflated land prices. Furthermore, relief mechanisms for those not allowed to build should also be provided.

In general, urban service areas should:

1. be part of a comprehensive planning process that addresses more than just the urban service area concept with housing, environmental, and transportation plans supplementing the urban service area plan, not being replaced by it;
2. be based upon a realistic service boundary, which represents the

community's needs, the locality's fiscal capacity, and the physical features of the land;

3. be subject to an annual review procedure to allow changes in the environment to be accommodated within the system.
4. be designated with allowance made for surplus land areas, to avoid the potential high demand and restricted supply problems which might drive up the cost of housing;
5. be established with a formal relief petition so that aggrieved landowners can request a change from the planning agency and not have to go to court; and
6. control those services either actually or by an expressed agreement with the agency to which it conditions development. Otherwise the purpose of the system is defeated and many landowners are unduly impacted.

Though, thus far, the majority of interest in the service area comes from county jurisdictions, the Colorado Legislature entertained legislation which would have allowed cities to condon off such areas. The defeated bill would have authorized service boundaries, provided they reflected social, economic, and physical capacities of the target areas. Under the bill, open space preserved in that land outside the designated area could only be used in agricultural, recreational, and rural capacities. Additionally, new cities could not have been incorporated within the service areas of existing cities, nor could special service districts be formed.[1]

A version of this policy at the local level is found in Manatee County, Florida. The optimum population and urban growth plan (OPUG) is based upon a flexible limitation line. Portions identified as existing urban areas will be afforded public service extensions aimed at successive ring expansion from these cores. Development is not allowed unless infrastructure capacity exists or the developer agrees to install such at his own expense. The process occurs in five-year increments, providing that by 1987, the limit line will encompass the current reserve area.[2]

Defining the boundary is the hardest task, drawing on the planner's ability to analyze demographic data and integrate it within the broader planning process. The community's needs and resources should be drawn upon in an effort to delineate a realistic boundary line.

The Eugene-Springfield, Oregon system exemplifies this approach. As one element in its 1990 plan, a compact growth form was devised. In order to develop an infrastructure capacity boundary, a natural features inventory was conducted, augmented with employment, population, and service projections. The anticipated 1990 area represents the geographic space within which a minimum level of services will be provided. Flexibility and accountability are retained by annual reviews to insure the adequacy of the program.[3] If substantial changes occur, initial calculations can be revised. Instead of a fragmented approach to land use, Eugene-Springfield identified its goals, implemented a method based upon social and economic constraints of attaining these goals, and continually updates its system via annual reviews. The service area approach is more socially amenable than other methods such as moratoria and cap rates for it does not purport to limit or freeze growth; rather it attempts to rationally stage future expansion. Again, it implements a policy designed to ameliorate "leap frog" development patterns since municipal services will not be extended beyond the boundary.

While the Eugene-Salem approach does mandate continual reevaluation, there is no mechanism to provide relief for those developers or landowners who are unfairly burdened with excessive regulations. Furthermore, by spatially restricting housing supply, housing prices can become escalated.

To overcome these problems, Sacramento County, California devised a system to prevent haphazard conversion of land, yet mitigate against socially restrictive outcomes of the plan. Concerned with spiraling growth and the loss of prime agricultural lands, Sacramento's plan was to link future land use decisions with a service area specified in the general plan.[4] A detailed needs and resources inventory set the parameters for the boundary line; however, a comfortable 27 percent excess land margin was included in designating the service area to minimize potential supply-demand problems. Additionally, the remaining undeveloped areas were identified as agriculture reserve, to provide additional acreage if the service area could not meet anticipated needs. An annual review plus a thorough five to seven year reevaluation was devised to insure adherence, yet flexibility, to major policy determinations.

Unlike the Eugene-Salem system, if individuals find the Sacramento County's plan classifications objectionable, there is a formal mechanism to petition the governing body to release additional reserve land if it can be demonstrated that:

1. There has been substantial consumption of vacant land for development purposes, such that the amount of vacant land available for urban uses is insufficient to allow for the continued development of a full range of living environment.
2. For some other reason, additional land should be made available for urban development in order to achieve the goals and objectives outlined in the plan.

The Sacramento County Planning Commission can weigh these petitions against the plan in making a determination of whether the extension is justifiable. This is an important element, for once community goals are articulated and a formal procedure exists for relaxing the plan's requirements, planners can more precisely weigh the benefits of allowing the variation versus the impact it will have on the land use system. If a deviation is granted, it is based on an analysis of the capacity of the land use system. If a request is denied, the denial is also based on a similar analysis. Without such a review and appeal procedure, discontented landowners or developers would go directly to court, circumventing the planning process. As it turned out, two suits were brought against the commission by the McKeon Construction Company. After being denied subdivision approval for a 2,700 acre tract outside the cordoned area, McKeon Construction initiated an $80 million suit in April, 1972; the suit was dismissed for lack of cause. This was followed by a $40 million claim, asserting that the planning department conspired to prevent the company from developing its property. Again, the judge found that the plaintiff construction company provided insufficient evidence and should either submit further documentation or withdraw the suit.[5]

Returning to the actual plan, another advantage of the Sacramento approach was the establishment of a realistic boundary, based on projections of population and infrastructure capacity needs to 1990 by ten-year increments and then allowing a substantial surplus. To avoid creating supply and demand problems, it is essential that the service area not be too small. Where supply is restricted but demand is not, it would be expected that land prices would rise, at least for those types of land especially suited for development.

Committing a reasonable supply of developable land laced with adequate facilities is desirable as long as the governing entity controls those services to which it conditions development.[6] Speculating that other agencies—schools, parks, or utilities—will be responsive to boundary plans is too uncertain, placing an undue burden upon those awaiting development permission based on anticipated service capacity. This is the defect in the Eugene-Springfield plan. It is hard to rationalize how a planning board can disapprove a plan based on service inadequacies when the local governing body does not have the power to eventually supply the needed services. Such provisions represent permanent injunctions against future development and cannot be countenanced.

An approach which reduces this possibility has been adopted on a regional scale by the Twin Cities Metropolitan Council. Responding to spiraling infrastructure costs, neighborhood deterioration, and a general deterioration in the quality of life, a development framework plan was devised.[7] The notion was that the area's geographic limits would be divided into eight sectors, each containing equal amounts of land and infrastructure capacity. Within these areas, two types of uses would be identified: urban service area—the portion which governmental agencies should plan to support development and to provide the necessary public facilities and services; and rural service area—the portion which will not receive major urban services until 1990.[9]

Further delineation of the urban service component specified developmentally ripe areas by five-year increments (1975-1990). Residential, commercial, and industrial needs were estimated for the five-year period and this data was integrated with public facility plans, to arrive at the extent and location of developable land. Ensuring that enough land plus five additional years' supply was to be available within each sector, and that environmentally sensitive and prime agricultural lands were not included within the available supply were two critical considerations in establishing the boundary lines.

The five-year excess capacity margin was included to prevent land price inflation as well as to accommodate slight variations in the projected growth rates. To further insure the integrity of the planning process, the council, through its regional land use power, mandated:

1. overall development in the area will be coordinated through shared planning and implementation responsibilities. This includes that counties, municipalities, and school boards prepare and adopt detailed comprehensive plans that are consistent with and help promote the Metropolitan Development Guide.
2. a capital improvement program covering sewers, transportation, and open space will be developed and updated at least every four years.
3. tax benefits should accrue to those who keep their land undeveloped in a manner compatible with land use regulations.[9]

While this approach addresses some of the deficiencies previously alluded to, the major limiting feature of service area strategies is the inability to time expansion. Urban service plans do not have any provisions which control the rate that population will be absorbed. Sequencing is addressed, but the amount of population to be assimilated is left to market forces. In the next chapter we will discuss a technique aimed at limiting population levels —the cap rate.

NOTES

1. Bill Number 1092, *Zoning Digest,* Volume 27 (1975), p. 5.
2. American Law Institute and American Bar Association, *Local Government Policies for Urban Development—A Review of the State of the Art,* American Law Institute and American Bar Association Course of Study—Land Planning Regulation of Development (New Orleans: American Law Institute and American Bar Association, 1975), p. 167.
3. Lane Council of Governments, *1990 Plan, Eugene-Springfield Metropolitan Area* (Eugene, Oregon: Lane Council of Governments, 1972), pp. 13-14.
4. Sacramento County, California, *Explanation of the County's Controlled Growth Policy and the Function of Reserve Areas,* Sacramento County Inter-Departmental Correspondence, 1975.
5. Michael Gleeson et al., "Urban Growth Management Systems," *Planning Advisory Service.* Report Numbers 309-310 (Chicago: American Society of Planning Officials, 1975), p. 24.
6. American Law Institute and American Bar Association, *Local Government Policies* p. 188.
7. Metropolitan Council of the Twin Cities, *Development Framework: Policy, Plan, Program* (St. Paul, Minnesota: Metropolitan Council of the Twin Cities, 1975).
8. *Ibid.,* pp. 16-19.
9. *Ibid.,* pp. 50-52.

Chapter Seven:
Cap Rates

Several municipalities have placed absolute ceilings—cap rates—on population. While theoretically cap rates are very appealing, their practical application has been less impressive. First, it is questionable to what degree of precision future population projections can be derived. Even if they can be reasonably precise, flexibility or the capacity to respond to changing circumstances is severely limited. Typically, the levels articulated are in response to impressions of an appropriate ceiling. The practice has been that the cap rate is set and the controls are then devised to support the system. Obviously, this is a highly questionable approach. However, a more significant flaw in the use of cap rates is the lack of any timing device. The assumption is that growth occurring within the jurisdiction will be uniform and continuous. However, demand may increase to the extent that the municipality is unable to accommodate it.

To reduce these adversities, agencies embarking on a total population charter provision should: determine the cap rate on the basis of empirically derived data; link the system with some timing control; and provide for a review procedure—assuring responsiveness to changing factors.

Despite the fact that the setting of cap rates violates the planning notion that you cannot quota development, a few municipalities have turned to the cap rate as a management tool. Boulder, Colorado explored using a population ceiling in conjunction with other growth control strategies. During citizen examination of alternative planning strategies, the People to Reclaim the Environment (PURE) conducted citizen preference surveys and found that three-quarters of the inhabitants favored placing a population ceiling at 100,000. The local chapter of Zero Population Growth collected enough signatures to place this issue on the 1971 ballot. Reacting to this, the Boulder City Council formulated an alternative resolution to examining the issue of growth with its attendant impacts.[1] Subsequently, the charter amendment to limit population to 100,000 was defeated by a 20 percent margin (60-40) while the council support measure passed 70-30. (The open space strategy discussed in chapter 1 evolved from the council's study.)

A more renowned charter provision was passed in Boca Raton, Florida. Like Boulder, Boca Raton embraced an open space procurement policy, but the main focus of the growth control scheme revolved around limiting future building permits to 40,000. Applying a household multiplier slightly greater than 2.5, this 40,000 cap would allow for approximately 105,000 additional residents, a number deemed compatible with Boca's way of life. In a law suit filed by the Arvida Corporation against the city, the circuit court found this provision unconstitutional, as opinion affirmed by the district court of appeals.[2]

One study has noted that to be litigation-proof, the quota needs to be periodically reviewed—something that Boca did not prescribe—to insure flexibility within the planning process.[3] Even this requirement misses the point. Setting such a quota is analogous to end-state planning. It is unrealistic to think that optimum population levels can be determined. In this regard, the Boca and Boulder efforts do not deserve serious consideration. While Boca used its planning apparatus to initiate "cap implementation levels," based on an arbitrary 105,000 ceiling, which lacked any empirical justification. More importantly, the setting of cap rates, as well as the designation of urban service areas, is devoid of timing provisions. How and when are additional individuals going to be assimilated within the area's social, economic, and political fabric? The necessity to sequence and locate development is not addressed by either of these methods.

The cap rates in Boca Raton were set in response to public attitudes or perceptions of growth. While citizen participation is an integral part of the planning process, the effort in Boca represents parochial community attitudes, in complete disregard of trends within the region. The absurdity of this approach is surpassed in St. Petersburg's population hoax. Concerned with increased impact on city services and facilities, the city council passed a maximum population level of 235,000 in March 1974. However, the existing population surpassed this figure by 25,000, with housing providing for 7,000 more people already underway. The ordinance, as passed by the city council 4-3, retroactively established the population level at 225,000, effective January 1, 1973. Persons moving to the city since then (1973) would have to register with the city, stating the time of their arrival. The first 10,000 individuals would be classified as permanent residents (225,000 plus 10,000 to equal the 235,000 ceiling), the remaining 25,000 (the 260,000-235,000) would be classified as temporary residents. This "surplus," plus anyone desiring to move there, would file applications to become replacements for those permanent residents who either died or relocated. On second consideration, the proposal was soundly defeated, as it was revealed that this proposition was a "tongue in cheek" counter to a recently enacted moratorium on new development.[4]

To reiterate, if municipalities are to embark on a successful cap rate strategy, the population ceiling must be based on rigorous empirical evidence and not on subjective community perceptions about future growth. More importantly, some form of timing provision needs to be embraced to avoid discontinuous growth patterns. Additionally, to ensure against faulty cap projections, an annual review procedure must be established and integrated with the cap rate strategy.

Annual permit limitations, which we will turn to now, is an approach which attempts to justify development quotas and alleviate some of the loopholes in current cap rate strategies.

NOTES

1. Earl Finkler and David Peterson, *Nongrowth Planning Strategies: The Developing Power of Towns, Cities and Regions* (New York: Praeger Publishers, 1974), pp. 27-42.
2. Arvida Corporation v. City of Boca Raton 312 So. 2d 826 (1975).
3. Michael Gleeson et al., "Urban Growth Management Systems," *Planning Advisory Service,* Report Numbers 309 and 310 (Chicago: American Society of Planning Officials, 1975), p. 46.
4. "St. Petersburg Council Votes To Cut Back Population," *New York Times,* March 26, 1974, p. 24.

Chapter Eight:
Annual Permit Limitations

E stablishing an annual limitation on building permits is basically a rationing scheme, authorizing a specified number of building permits annually. It is different from the cap rate in that it attempts to justify its quota, granting development permission after the plans have met certain infrastructure and aesthetic criteria. As such, it is a direct means of control over both the magnitude and location of growth.

The uniqueness of the annual permit limitation approach is that proposals are evaluated collectively. Unlike the traditional system in which applications are acted upon individually and in disregard to others, this mechanism holds a competition whereby all projects compete against each other for the allotted permits. While under considerable attack for its apparent defiance of market factors, the annual permit limitation method does attempt to justify approval or denial of project applications. Under the conventional zoning process, where denials are seldom justified, the permit limitation technique advances the reasons behind disallowance—with these decisions open to public scrutiny and debate.

Caution needs to be exercised so that the quota and conditioning factors are realistic and take into account regional dynamics. They should not be veils for exclusionary practices. Another problem may arise if the municipality fails to commit the finances necessary to provide the services to which development is conditioned. The governmental agency cannot absolve itself of its responsibility by forcing the developer to provide everything in terms of additional services. Aesthetic controls should also be used with caution so that they are not given too much weight in the evaluation process. While the municipality has a right to want and require visually appealing projects, the subjective nature of aesthetic criteria needs to be recognized.

The following may serve as useful guidelines for establishing annual permit limitations:

1. Quota should be realistic and not merely an exclusionary device.
2. A municipal financial commitment is necessary to provide the services to which the development is conditioned.
3. An annual review procedure should exist to evaluate the effectiveness of the program.

Pleasanton, California provides one example of an annual permit limitation policy. Apprehensive about losing its small town atmosphere, open space, and relatively low taxes, the municipality conditioned building permits upon sewer capacity. Three-hundred building permits were initially allotted on the basis of the local treatment plant's capability. Projected 1975-1976 capacities allowed an additional 500 annual permits, bringing the level to 800, the amount adopted by the city council.[1]

Returning to two strategies mentioned in Chapter 3, the cities of New Castle, New York and Marlboro, New Jersey developed formulas specifying the number of permits allowed. In reviewing the New Castle formula—which allowed only 112 annual building permits on any land declared to be within a special residence district—the court found the regulation arbitrary and without any statutory authority: "There is nothing in Town Law 261 that gives the defendant town power to regulate the rate of its growth and the Zoning Ordinance Article under attack here is a direct regulation of the rate of growth and nothing more."[2] Without any assurance that the formula was drawn in accordance with any plan to facilitate the adequate provision of necessary facilities, the court concluded that since the permit limitations *solely* addressed the rate of growth, and not its sequence, the provision could not be justified.

Bothered by the absence of a linkage between the plan and any serious documentation, the court in the Marlboro case[3] found the ten-permit "step-wise" provision to be *ultra vires* and unconstitutional. Continuing on, the judiciary cautioned against "drastic" arrangements which would disrupt normal construction practice and impinge on the industry's business—so long as the plans and specifications have met local requirements.

Completing a tri-state effort, Enfield, Connecticut enacted an ordinance enabling planned development via special permit. Under one such permit, it was deemed that no more than 375 apartment units could be accommodated. After the first 212 units had been approved, plaintiff DeMaria petitioned the town for the remaining allotments. Denied building permission, DeMaria instituted legal proceedings. In the meantime, the planning board gave the CDIC Corporation permission to build the 112 units. Angered at the town's unreasonable treatment of DeMaria, the court ruled in favor of the plaintiff, enabling him to eventually secure his project.[4]

Though all three of the previous cases were invalidated on different grounds, Norman Williams has pointed out that any attempt to ration building permits should be supported with empirical evidence demonstrating both the public purpose served and the appropriateness of the remedy.[5] The now famed Petaluma plan is based on such a process. Burdened with enormous municipal expansion, potentially outdistancing infrastructure capacities, Petaluma adopted a policy to "control the quality, distribution and rate of growth of the city."[6] Located in the northern part of California, Petaluma experienced relatively small amount of growth—4,000 from 1950—bringing the 1960 population level to 14,000. With the construction of Highway 101, bisecting Petaluma Valley, San Francisco became commutable, enabling an additional 5,000 inhabitants to spill into Petaluma during the last half of the 1960 decade. This cycle climaxed in late 1971 with the arrival of 5,000 new residents since 1970. To complicate this pattern, there was a discontinuity in the distribution of homes, with the eastern section of the municipality receiving the majority of new units. To attempt to remedy this imbalance, and to avoid the projected population increase, studies of infrastructure capacity were initiated; a moratorium was placed on rezoning, annexation, and development, and a series of meetings were held, in addition to a residential preference survey.

These events refined the comprehensive planning process and produced a new housing element of the general plan and an environmental design program. The outcome of these measures culminated in 1972 with the adoption of the Petaluma Residential Development Control System. This system provides a formal mechanism to implement policy deliberations articulated in the general, housing, and environmental documents. More specifically, the system establishes annual numerous single and multi-family quotas, for the 1973-1977 period, and then provides for spatial distribution of these units in the various sectors of the city. Supplementing these quantity and distribution specifications, the city council is empowered to stipulate that, in any year, between 8 and 12 percent of the annual quota be available for low- and moderate-income housing.[7]

To oversee and administer the development control system, a residential development evaluation board was established. Based on the allocation quotas detailed by the city council—at least three months prior to the September 1 development application deadline—the board reviews the prospective developments and makes development permission recommendations, reevaluating, upon the request of the developer, any proposal not receiving any development privileges. These findings are then forwarded to the city council, which ultimately grants the development allotments.

Petaluma's development allotment program requires preliminary municipal approval *before* a builder can apply for traditional plat and building permit permission. In addition to evaluating the application for standard specifications—site utilization and development, preliminary architectural and landscaping schemes and a housing market analysis—the board evaluates the proposed development in relation to its conformity with the general, housing, and environmental planning studies. If the proposal reinforces and is consistent with these documents, it is then examined in terms of its impact upon public facilities and services. The impact upon the local infrastructure is measured and numerically articulated as a function of the following criteria:

1. Capacity of the water system to serve the proposed development;
2. The efficiency of the sanitary sewers to handle site effluents;
3. Ability of drainage facilities to absorb surface run-off;
4. The capacity of the fire department to respond to an on-site emergency without jeopardizing residents' health, safety, or welfare;
5. The absorption of new students from the proposed development by the school system;
6. The capacity of existing road and park systems to accommodate cars and persons generated by the new development.[8]

The assignment of a maximum of thirty points—a possible five points for each of the six categories—is apportioned upon compliance of at least two-thirds of the members of the board, voting on each criteria. In other words, if two-thirds of the members assign the particular variable five points, it is credited with a score of five. If this test cannot be met, then the element receives zero points.

The last technique used in evaluating the project concerns the quality of its design and its contribution to public welfare and amenity. Accordingly, these criteria are composed of:

1. Site and architectural design quality, indicated by the harmony of the proposed building, exemplified with size, height, color and location with existing neighborhood development;
2. Site and architectural quality shown by the building promoting sound circulation (on- and off-site), safety and privacy;
3. Site and architectural quality manifested by the amount and character of the landscaping and screening;
4. The provision of public and/or private usable open space and/or pathways along the Petaluma riverway and creeks;
5. Contributions to and extensions of existing foot, bicycle, equestrian trails, and the green belt provided for in the environmental design plan;
6. The provision of needed public facilities such as critical linkages in the major street system, school rooms or other vital public facilities;

7. The extent to which the proposed development accomplishes an orderly and contiguous extension of existing development as against leapfrog expansion;
8. The provision of units to meet the city's policy goal of 8 to 12 percent low- and moderate-income dwelling units annually.[9]

Applying a zero to ten scale to these variables, the votes are tabulated and then divided by the number of members voting to determine an application's point specification. Points for the public facility availability and the quality of design and contribution to public welfare and amenity are totaled separately and are then designated by housing type and geographical location. Applications which do not receive a minimum of twenty-five and fifty points from the respective two review categories are eliminated from any further allotment consideration.

Pursuant to the development allotment matrix, the remaining projects are awarded their allotments with the highest rankings in each category receiving such an assignment. This process is repeated until all 500 permits have been evaluated.[10]

These findings are then disseminated and a public hearing scheduled. If an applicant is dissatisfied with the numerical evaluation his application has received, he may request the residential development evaluation board to reevaluate its point total. If this reevaluation also proves to be unsatisfactory, the developer may submit a written notification of his dissent to the city council, prior to its action on developmental allotments.

Once the public hearing occurs, appeal or no appeal, the evaluations are transferred to the city council which is empowered to make the final allocations, completing the Petaluma mechanism.[11]

In adjudicating the suit brought by the construction industry, the district court found the City's plan to infringe upon the constitutionally guaranteed "right to travel." On appeal, the Ninth Circuit never reached this substantive issue of right to travel, rather overturned the lower court, finding the complainant lacking standing to obtain relief under the right to travel doctrine.[12]

Considering the previously discussed flaws in traditional zoning procedures which force developers to make agreements with the local governing body to secure project approval, one wonders why the Construction Industry Association of Sonoma County felt so threatened by Petaluma's plan. If it was the housing quota which was disturbing, Petaluma might have countered that municipalities have long found ways to perpetuate this under the guise of minimum acre zoning. The only difference being that the quota, and the criteria upon which it is based, are not articulated. Under the traditional system, a developer would come in and request a zoning change. The planning board, and ultimately the governing body, would review this request and render a decision without ever specifying the standards used in making its determination. The disparity in this approach was demonstrated in an adequate public facilities ordinance case. Fairfax County, Virginia denied rezoning permission to one individual and based its denial on inadequate service provisions. However, a neighboring property owner was able to secure rezoning. "The evidence introduced, and the argument advanced by the Board, that the county's public facilities would be unduly impacted by the Allman rezoning . . . was negated by a showing of the Board's other rezonings which had the same, or even greater, impact than would have resulted from the Allman development."[13] In successfully litigating this case, the plaintiff had to overcome the substantial presumption of the plan's validity to show that the local official acted unreasonably and arbitrarily. Had a system delineating criteria existed, Allman would have been provided with more substantive evidence of why he was refused, and secondly, even if he was unsatisfied with this outcome, it would have been much easier to show capricious actions against the board.

In the Petaluma case, a second concern of the Construction Industry Association of Sonoma County was the restraint on the number of building permits allocated. Though more permits were awarded in the previous two years, the 1967-1971 average annual amount fell below the 500 level.[14] "Even if Petaluma was adopted to curb the natural growth rate to some extent, it is still better than conventional zoning when it is employed for the same purpose. Here when a quota is established it is not articulated, so one cannot even debate whether it is rational. Furthermore, if any standards are used for allocating the hidden quota they are not only arbitrary but in many cases venal."[15]

The novel feature in the Petaluma system is its method for ascertaining development permission. Unlike present practices in which proposals are acted upon without regard to others, Petaluma requires a competition. This gives the city the opportunity to evaluate and select projects receiving high proximity and aesthetic point totals. Surely the construction industry, diehards of the free market, cannot find this objectionable. What is troublesome, and something the Construction Industry Association of Sonoma County did not challenge, is the Catch-22 method of apportioning points. Too much weight is given to the less precise, aesthetic variables. Also, the infrastructure distribution of points should not be assigned on an all-or-nothing basis. Some interim scaling should be provided.

When evaluated in terms of its intent, the Petaluma plan reveals another deficiency. The objective of the five-year plan was to balance discontinuous development that had put the majority of new construction in the eastern portion of the county. When first year allocations were made, the following distribution was evident:

Sector and Configuration	*Quota*	*Request*	*Allocation*
Eastside, multifamily	125	256	125
Eastside, single family	125	505	125
Westside, multifamily	130	59	59
Westside, single family	120	118	118
Totals	500	938	427

The city allocated only 85 percent of its permits. The western section, the area in which growth was to be redistributed, has 73 (250 less 177) unutilized permits. Simply singling out the western sector to be developed does not insure policy effectuation. Incentives such as using the discretionary 10 percent quota modification as a reward for developing in specified areas could be an effective remedy, without jeopardizing the whole program.

A design similar to the Petaluma program was used in Pitkin County, Colorado. With Aspen located within its confines, the county has experienced sizable annual growth rates. Noting that while first generation tools strengthened with environmental controls have helped, they "do not prevent against a sudden burst of growth reminiscent of development pressures in the years from 1967-1972."[16] Therefore, the thrust of Pitkin County's plan is to produce a "rationale and administrative implementation mechanism for an annual growth rate."[17] Hence, a slightly altered Petaluma version has been proposed. While in this instance the county's efforts are based on its own planning needs, adoption of another agency's program simply because it has been legally validated cannot be countenanced. Each municipality has its own social and economic fabric and the plan needs to be responsive to it.

Under the Pitkin plan the county is divided into twelve sectors. Each area is evaluated and assigned an annual percent allocation. For areas that have had recent population projection updates, varied household sizes, according to the type of land use permitted, were applied to these 1985 levels and brought up to date to determine the yearly allotment. In areas not covered by the master plan, a 3 percent annual growth rate was applied to the extant stock to produce its annual limit. Then all development applications were collected by September 1 and evaluated collectively using the criteria and point system adopted by Petaluma, the only difference being that the 0-5 infrastructure points are not given on an all-or-nothing basis. The applicants receiving the highest scores are then allocated their permits until the annual number is exhausted. The only difference here is that with 1,179 officially subdivided lots, allocations to previously approved projects retain priority. In fact, they need not even go through the point system for the ordinance cannot apply retrospectively.[18]

Once permit approval has been granted, construction is to initiate within sixty days, otherwise the county commissioner retains the right to rescind all or part of the allotment. The rationale here probably parallels that previously discussed in the chapter on interim development controls—namely, to prevent a "race of diligence." This protects the town from the abuse of developers obtaining permits and holding them as a hedge against future county actions. However, unlike the year or two conscription associated with the interim controls, sixty days seems an unreasonably short period of time for the developer to initiate construction. Securing financing, negotiating with contractors, and awaiting materials can inordinately delay even the most eager builder.

Unlike the experience with population caps, annual permit limitations do afford more rationality, although it might behoove local governments to specify standards (as opposed to numerical conditions) upon which development is permissible. A recurring problem in all annual permit methods is their inability to address the timing of development which is a necessary factor in any effective growth management strategy. To quote Norman Williams, "it is reasonable to assume that the rationing of building permits does not provide a satisfactory solution to this problem without a sequence dimension."[19] Such a strategy is embraced in the adequate facilities plan, the subject of the following section.

NOTES

1. Livingston and Blayney, *Pleasanton General Review: Alternative Growth Strategies, City of Pleasanton, California* (San Francisco: Livingston and Blayney, 1972).
2. Albrecht Realty Company, Inc. v. Town of New Castle 167 N.Y.S. 2d 843, 844 (1957).
3. U.S. Home and Development Corporation v. LaMura 214 A.2d 538 (1965).
4. DeMaria v. Enfield Planning and Zoning Commission 271 A.2d 105 (1970).
5. Norman Williams, *American Land Planning Law*, Vol. III (Chicago: Callaghan and Company, 1976), p. 353.
6. *Residential Development Control System of the City of Petaluma*, Resolution Number 6113, adopted by the city council, August, 1972.
7. Allotments were 40 and 61 for 1975-1976 and 1976-1977 respectively.
8. Residential Development Control System of the City of Petaluma.
9. *Ibid.*
10. In this fashion, a development may receive allotments even if it has fewer aggregate points than one rejected, if it is located in an area specifying more units to be built.
11. Construction Industry Association of Sonoma County v. City of Petaluma 375 F. Supp. 574 (1974).
12. Record Number 74-2100, August, 1975; regarding the implications of the Petaluma plan, I am indebted to comments offered by Professor Jan Krasnoweicki.
13. Board of Supervisors of Fairfax County v. Allman, Circuit Court of Fairfax County, Record Numbers 730991, and 74029, 1975, p. 13.

14. Year   Permits Granted
    1967   234
    1968   379
    1969   358
    1970   591
    1971   891
    The annual average from 1967-1971 is 491.
15. Jan Krasnowiecki, *Zoning Litigation: How To Win Without Really Losing,* Unpublished paper, University of Pennsylvania Law School, Philadelphia, Pennsylvania, 1975, p. 7.
16. *Pitkin County Growth Management Plan Draft,* Aspen-Pitkin County Planning Board, Aspen, Colorado, 1975, p. 1.
17. *Ibid.*
18. *Ibid.,* p. 18.
19. Williams, *American Land Planning,* p. 353.

Chapter Nine:
Adequate Public Facilities
Programming

Broadening the subdivision process, adequate public facilities programming seeks to guide development, making it consonant with the municipality's ability to accommodate growth. Distinct from the cap rate or annual permit limitation, this strategy emphasizes directing rather than retarding growth. As such, it is an indirect tool, aimed at the adequacy, rather than the magnitude of municipal expansion. Typically two types of programs emerge: limited phasing mechanisms, and expanded phasing mechanisms.

Under the limited phasing mechanisms, one or two service facilities—water, sewer, roads, schools, and so forth—are specified as the conditioning variables. In other words, the developer has to prove that his project is consistent with the specification prior to obtaining development approval. A disadvantage with this method is that frequently the limited mechanism is adopted in response to a temporary service inadequacy; thus, an elaborate procedure is developed around a specific, short-term problem. The project is not evaluated in its entirety, but rather on its deficiency in one or two areas. Such an inadequacy cannot be allowed to unilaterally enjoin what otherwise might be a sound project.

A typical scenario for the expanded mechanism would be the specification of a series of conditioning variables with the developer having to demonstrate adequacy in all cases before being allowed to proceed with conventional zoning and subdivision application review. These variables would then be financially backed, usually through a capital improvement program, to provide the requisite services over time—at the municipality's absorption level.

A potential problem arising here is that the municipality often does not control the services upon which it predicates the development. Schools, sewers, and other infrastructure are often in special districts or reside with some other authority. It is an arrogant policy to disallow development without having the capacity to remedy that which caused the denial of the project. Other problems concern the control of only residential use, and the imposition of a system on top of an already exclusionary strategy. Wanting to curb growth, but only focusing upon the residential element, is like saying "it is o.k. for you to work here but not to live here."

Many programs offer relief mechanisms if the capital improvement program deviates from schedule. Allowing the developer to build in the year the plan shows he will have adequate service facilities, regardless of whether the capacity exists or not, is legally expeditious but antithetical to the overall program. An additional obstruction occurs when, under the guise of reducing sprawl, facilities are programmed; without any mechanism to cluster development, the final land use form is just as discontinuous and more costly to service. The municipality gets locked into a static system and central program elements are lost. To avoid such an outcome, a more responsive system should encompass:

1. An adequate facilities plan as part of the comprehensive planning process linking infrastructure extensions with housing, transportation, and environmental elements;
2. A governmental agency which controls the facilities to which development is conditioned;
3. A realistic capital improvement plan which can be implemented on schedule, reducing deviations;
4. Control of all types of development, not just residential;
5. A plan which takes the natural features of the land into account;
6. An annual review or update mechanism to periodically evaluate and, perhaps, redesign the plan.

The second generation system that has received the most use, recognition, and legitimization in this regard is the so-called adequate public facilities (APF), phased growth, or timing and sequential controls (TASC) ordinance. While other measures have directly tried to limit growth, the APF approach seeks to guide development, making it consonant with municipal infrastructure availability. At best, this linkage enables growth to be encouraged in serviceable areas, staving off development in remote, unserviceable locales. Specifically, TASCs attempt to prevent development from outstripping the municipality's ability to provide basic services and, secondly, limit excess subdivision with its attendant ills.

Within these confines, three basic methods are possible: regulation of overall development rates; regulation of the geographical development sequence; and regulation designed to maintain a balance among various types of uses.

While current developments have thrust the APF ordinances into the planning limelight, phasing is not a new idea. Twenty years ago, the town of Milford, Connecticut embarked upon such a program. The municipality had practically exhausted its borrowing ability and sought to bring development in line with the municipality's ability to plan, design, finance, and construct such improvements. A subdivision priority map was devised which illustrated high and low development priority areas. Applications for development within a low priority area were required to demonstrate that:

1. At least one existing street leading from the subdivision to the high priority area was of sufficient width, suitable grade and alignment, suitably improved, and suitably located to accommodate the prospective increased traffic and to provide adequate means of access for fire fighting.
2. The existing sanitary sewer mains and sewage disposal facilities or water mains and water pumping facilities or storm water drains were adequate to accommodate the additional demand that would be created by the subdivision.
3. The public elementary school system, either existent or approved construction, was adequate to accommodate the prospective number of school age children who would be likely to live in the subdivision.

If a service inadequacy existed, but all other compliance is fulfilled, subdivision approval might be conditioned to a development timetable. Such a schedule would phase a minimum of 20 percent of the lots shown on the approved plan, over a maximum five-year period. This enabled Milford to plan and construct its infrastructure on a somewhat parallel rate with new construction. An alternative relief procedure allowed the developer to advance the project date by putting in the requisite facilities at his expense. In applying this voluntary procedure, the subdivision regulations defined standards guiding conversion of land into a higher priority area.

A similar program was adopted around the same time in Clarkstown, New York. Feeling development pressure, the Clarkstown Zoning Ordinance created a concentric circle expansion pattern around the old county seat of New City, and along a corridor extending south to the intersection of the Palisades Parkway and the New York State Thruway. The orientation of this plan was to direct development toward these areas. The inner ring, closest to the city, was zoned for immediate suburban development at 15,000-square-foot lots subsequently enlarged to 22,500-square-foot. Open space and larger land areas were reserved at 1-acre lots in the outer ring with the thrust of the management program focusing on the intermediate ring. This area was zoned "special district" with residential development proceeding on one-acre parcels. However, the town board was authorized to relax this requirement, permitting 15,000-square-foot plats upon a showing that none of the infrastructure systems, especially the schools, would be adversely impacted. The refusal of a special permit for the 15,000 square-foot lot in the intermediate ring triggered litigation, with the validity of the town's refusal and the legality of the whole program upheld.[2]

Though important parts of the Clarkstown mechanism were removed in 1963, Norman Williams, in evaluating the decennial (1955-1965) progress of the plan, noted that: (a) The predominant development pattern in Clarkstown was in fact concentrated in the area surrounding New City, and in the corridor extending south toward the interchange, and (b) Subdivisions approved in the earlier years were closer in, nearer the older settlement in New City, and the location of such subdivisions tended to move farther out as time went on.[3]

However, Williams also noted that up until 1965 there was not any intrusion of higher density zoning and development into the large area designated for permanent acreage development north of New City. Since vacant land was being quickly depleted, the pressure to rezone to smaller lots would be manifest, possibly jeopardizing the objectives of the plan.[4]

A geographical management public facilities program was adopted in St. Louis, Missouri. The metropolitan area was experiencing unprecedented growth with the western sector rapidly approaching its saturation point. When the application of a first generation program, 3-acre minimum lot sizes, failed to reduce development pressure, the planning commission sought to affect the type and rate of growth. Developable and nondevelopable surbareas were delineated, accompanied with criteria indicating minimal location considerations before any subarea could be recommended for intensified use. The school, sewer, drainage, utility, and transportation standards that were set formed the plan's basis.[5]

Brooklyn Park, Minnesota similarly addressed geographical disparity in development. Determined to prevent development north of a major through arterial, the city enacted agricultural and minimum lot rezoning to redirect growth southward. The failure to accomplish this manifested in a requirement that any proposed subdivision north of 85th Avenue have available or provide its own off-site drainage system. This stipulation was later broadened, leading to a 1972 schedule of timing and extent of municipal service provisions.[6]

The Prince Georges County, Maryland approach touches both the overall and geographical balancing methods. Based on annual population and employment targets, growth is to be channeled toward areas already served or programmed for service. This proposed staging plan divides the county into development districts with "economic potential sectors" designed to assist in the balancing of the tax base and home-work mix. The remaining areas are designated to encourage development, limit it, or defer it altogether.[7]

Another overall development regulatory system is found in Livermore, California. A 1960-1970 doubling of the city's population manifested in an annual 1,500 building permit limitation to only those lots already existing on the record. The insufficiency and haste of this enactment gave way to a management strategy specifying education, sewage, and water performance standards. Future residential apportionments were prohibited until satisfactory solutions could be provided for the following stipulations:

1. Education Facilities: no double sessions in schools nor overcrowded classrooms as determined by the California Educational Code.
2. Sewage: the sewage· treatment facilities and capacities must meet the Regional Water Quality Control Board's standards.
3. Water Supply: no water rationing with respect to human consumption or irrigation and adequate fire protection reserves must exist.[8]

Aside from the poor and ambiguous drafting of this ordinance, an administrative agency empowered to assess insufficiencies and carry out solutions was not established. Livermore makes a hollow request by not providing any planning or financial commitments. Furthermore, the ordinance attempts to control an action which, in California, is considered ministerial. Once a plan has been approved by respective agencies, the granting of a building permit is a nondiscretionary action. The permit granting agency is not authorized to evaluate a plan's impacts in light of municipal policies. That is the job of the review agencies.

A modified timing and sequencing plan conditions expansion to the provision of one specified facility. One such plan is that in Pinellas County, Florida, which conditions development upon adequate water facilities. Drought coupled with accelerated growth led the county to devise a plan for allocating water, using an algebraic equation encompassing four impact variables —population distribution, rate of growth, land area, and assessed valuation. Under the model, each governmental body within the county is assigned its percentage of water allocation, with this amount controlling the number of building permits issued.[9]

Milpitas, California uses school capacity as its central variable. The purpose of the Milpitas' Residential Regulatory Formula Ordinance is to measure residential development on the basis of the ratio between school tax rates and school population. The formula specifies the maximum number of permits awarded. Residential proposals, stratified by pupils generated from each project, are then matched against these parameters to adetermine if development is permissible.[10]

A neighboring California community, San Jose, uses a similar strategy. Concerned with the overcrowding of schools, San Jose enacted an initiative ordinance which forbids zoning actions by the city council, if the schools in the development's service area are saturated. Specifically, the three-tiered process first prohibits the council from zoning, prezoning, or rezoning any land for residential use if the projected enrollment of the proposed development will violate the following schedules:

Grade	Enrollment	Sq. Ft./Pupil
1–6	300	55
7–8	750	75
9–12	750	85

Proposals which do not affect school enrollment are exempted from the regulations. Otherwise, a developer must enter into an agreement with the school district to provide a satisfactory temporary alternative to permanent school construction, such as guaranteeing a line of credit to the school district, reimbursing it for any additional costs; delaying construction according to a timetable which will allow the district to provide permanent facilities; or dedicating land and/or money.

The second element permits the school district to protest any council approval on the grounds of adverse impact on school facilities generated by the development. Only an affirmative vote by the city council—five out of seven votes—will override the school's objection. The final provision, and the one still in the planning stages, would direct a study to be made analyzing the problems associated with residential development.[11] Litigation brought by the local homebuilders' association was overruled at the trial level with the court finding nothing unreasonable in the city's regulations. The ruling was appealed and a decision from the California Supreme Court is pending.[12]

In assessing the viability of limited phasing mechanisms, one is struck with the fact that these development policies are not in response to social and economic consequences of suburban land conversion; rather they have surfaced as attempts to reduce public expenditures and/or halt environmental deterioration. While the latter are noble goals, it must be recognized that any attempt to condition expansion upon service provision must have a carefully developed and articulated plan as a precursor: "Absent such, manipulation is no easy solution but a mere aimless regulation of an already overregulated citizenry."[13]

Conditioning development to one authority is similarly detrimental. The planning process is multidimensional in nature. Enabling one agency, with authority over only one component, to have a veto over the whole system is irresponsible. Even more dangerous is allowing nonplanning agencies to sustain such a veto power. The school or water authorities have limited perspectives and expertise, antithetical to a comprehensive approach mandated by a complex and evolving society. It should be recognized that there are "multiple influences on urban growth patterns, so that it may become apparent in some cases that elements other than utility extensions or utility financing play a salient role in guiding growth."[14]

Aware of these limitations, many municipalities have adopted broader strategies. Typically, preliminary inventories highlight the jurisdiction's problem(s) and propose possible courses of action. In the case of adequate public facilities, a capital improvement program (CIP) can be adopted, scheduling selected physical plans and facilities over time. The CIP represents a programming of facilities based on an assessment of the community's infrastructure needs. Skirting local restrictions on adopting official operating budgets for no more than a year or two, the capital improvement program makes a longer range forecast of certain types of expenditures. The five- or six-year plan reinforces each year's officially adopted budget. Flexibility is retained by annual reevaluation, permiting adjustments necessitated by any reallocations of resources.[15]

Prince Georges County, Maryland passed its APF based on a capital improvement program in 1970. The theory was that the planning board must ascertain that sufficient services exist or are programmed for the proposal's area before preliminary plan approval. In making this determination, the board scrutinizes the project as to its:

1. Availability of existing or programmed sewer and water main capacity;
2. Potential effect on the efficient and economic operation of existing or programmed public facilities;
3. Extensions of sewage and water facilities through unsubdivided lands;
4. Location vis-a-vis articulated timing of facility plans;
5. Availability to adequate access roads; and
6. Availability to adequate fire, police, park, utility, and recreation services.[16]

Based upon these criteria, the planning board disapproved a plan for the subdivision of two parcels. In seeking a writ of mandamus, and a mandatory injunction against such activities, Helen Rosenberg convinced the Maryland Court of Appeals that this regulation was arbitrary and capricious as applied.[17]

A companion case challenged the planning board's action when a preliminary plat was denied due to inadequate road facilities. In assessing varied contentions, Judge Mathias dismissed the plaintiff's taking and inadequate standard ascertains, but found the planning board's rulings unreasonable based on the facts.[18] Despite invalidations of these cases, neighboring Montgomery County, Maryland embarked upon a similar program.

The Premature Subdivision Ordinance and the Wedges and Corridors Plan of 1967 served as prerequisites to a more refined adequate public facilities ordinance in 1973. Montgomery County recognized that the provision of public services should be an integral part of the review and approval process. However, the state-imposed sewer moratorium created administrative difficulties for the county. Plats were continually being filled, necessitating subdivision processing. The result was that if approval was secured, the developer would have to wait until the moratorium was rescinded. The time lag between this lifting and the review procedure resulted in a proliferation of "nonconforming uses" due to intervening plan revisions. Subsequently, the planning board sought to control this situation by requiring the presence of infrastructure capability as a condition to plat approval. This would guard against circumventions of the sewer moratorium and, simultaneously, give the county time to consolidate its management strategy. Capacity levels were formalized along the proceeding lines:

1. Access Systems: a plan of mass transportation must exist or be planned within one-third of a mile; highways in the area must be able to accommodate projected traffic.
2. Water and Sewer: adequate systems must be available or be planned within two years; if they are unavailable, the developer may provide them subject to Maryland State Department of Health regulations. Septic systems are permissible if in accord with the Maryland or Montgomery County code, whichever is more stringent.
3. Roads: the systems within the subdivision must be adequate to accommodate emergency vehicles; fragmentation of street patterns must be avoided. The street lay-out must not be detrimental to reasonable development of adjacent lands.
4. Community Services and Facilities: schools and police must be available or scheduled to provide adequate and timely service to the subdivision.[19]

If the application is not approved, the developer may provide the necessary facilities. However, future vested rights, allowing a developer to build in the future if services are programmed for this area, are not granted. Augmenting this mechanism, a housing element is designed to assist in the provision of low- and moderate-income housing. Ordinance 7-53, passed in 1973, rewards builders of low-cost housing with a density increase of not more than 20 percent for a 25 percent low-income commitment. This was partially superseded by the requirement that any development exceeding fifty dwellings set aside 15 percent moderately priced units. While this recognition of housing need is commendable, placing the burden of providing low- and moderate-income housing entirely on the private sector is an abrogation of public responsibility. Low-income quotas absent any active municipal effort is not a solution. At least if the responsibility is to be shifted to the developer, an incentive option is preferable. The triggering of a low- and middle-housing commitment on the 50-unit level is arbitrary, bearing no reasonable relationship to the type of project. A 50-unit, single-family subdivision has different moderate-housing implications than a more intensive 50-unit configuration. If a threshold is to exist, it should be a function of intensity of use versus a simple arithmetic delineation.

A more advantageous approach would be an affirmative local program. Brooklyn Park, Minnesota has consciously embraced an inclusionary program in its developable area. The city encouraged multifamily dwellings, now constituting half of the city's housing stock. Moreover, both 235 and 236 scattered housing has been built. Augmenting this, the city council has approved plats relaxing many normal subdivision requirements to further benefit low-cost housing.

A major disadvantage of the Montgomery County program is the nonenumeration of the requisite administrative and compliance procedures. Also, under the water and sewer criteria, a three-tiered approval system was initiated: service approved by the county council; service approved by the county council within first two years, three to six years, and seven to ten years; service not approved. The drawback in this system is that the last classification can apply to any area regardless of the existence of service adequacy. Although a large portion of the county's land is covered under a twenty-year sewer program, a larger share has not been designated for service within ten years, with no major facility expansion planned.[20] Within the context of the county's refusal to extend development ahead of servicing, this could cause unreasonable and inequitable burdens on some landowners. A more equitable program exists in neighboring Fairfax County.

Beset with haphazard and irrevocably damaging growth, Fairfax County initiated a comprehensive evaluation of its planning and management mechanisms. The resulting PLUS program (Planning and Land Use System) sought to create a dynamic and responsive system. Specific policy objectives were:

1. To economize on the capital and operating costs of public facilities and services by carefully phasing residential development so as to be consonant with adequate and efficient provision of public improvements;
2. To establish and maintain county control over the character, direction, and timing of development;
3. To establish and maintain a desirable degree of balance among the various uses of land;
4. To establish and maintain essential quality of community services and facilities;
5. To preserve and protect open space land and agricultural, horticultural, and forest uses;
6. To preserve and protect the environment and environmentally critical areas; and
7. To preserve gasoline, heating fuel, and energy for vital public and private functions.[21]

From these objectives came a four-staged program consisting of an interim control program, a low- and moderate-income housing commitment, open space tax concessions, and a system of special permits for residential development. The residential development use permit mandates that prior to the issuance of any building permit or site plan approval, a residential developer is required to obtain a special permit stating the proximity of the project to specific municipal services. As such, this adequate facilities ordinance exists as a supplement to other programs. A Ramapo-like scaling system was developed, specifying that no special permit could be granted unless the development scored 22 points based on the following schedule:

	Points
Sewers	
Public sewers available	5
Package Sewer Plants	3
County approved septic system in R-C district	3
All others	0
Drainage	
Percentage of Required Drainage Capacity Available	
100 or more	5
90–99	4
80–89.9	3
65–79.9	2
50–64.9	1
Less than 50	0
Improved Park or Recreational Facility Including Public School	
Recreational Site	
Within 1/4 mile	5
Within 1/2 mile	3
Within 1 mile	1
Further than 1 mile	0
State, County, or Town Major, Secondary or Collector Road(s) Improved With Curbs and Sidewalks	
Direct Access	5
Within 1/2 mile	3
Within 1 mile	1
Further than 1 mile	0
Fire House	
Within 1 mile	3
Within 2 miles	1
Further than 2 miles	0
Police Station	
Within 2 miles	3
Within 4 miles	1
Further than 4 miles	0
Elementary School (with sufficient capacity to absorb the number of children expected to inhabit the development without resorting to double sessions or other methods to handle overcrowding)	
Within 1 mile	5
Within 1-1/3 miles	4
Within 2 miles	3
Within 2-1/2 miles	2
Within 3 miles	1
More than 3 miles	0

Additionally, a bonus was extended for low- and moderate-income units. Any residential developer who provided low- and moderate-income housing units in his development would receive the following bonus toward the 22 points required to obtain a special permit:

	Points
30% of total units	4
25% of total units	3
20% of total units	2
10% of total units	1
less than 10% of total units	0

The Fairfax County Capital Improvement Program delineated service extensions in accord with these breakdowns. In providing relief for those stringently bound by the plan, the county allows the builder to advance the project through: provision of requisite facilities; a variance from the strict application of the ordinance; or for those willing to forgo development submission, tax reductions. Despite these remedial provisions, two suits have been brought. In *Board of Supervisors of Fairfax County v. Allman,*[22] the petitioner failed to get a rezoning change, from single-family one per acre to three per acre. The board's contention was that the schools were not of such capacity to support the numbers of students generated by the proposed 988 units. The court came to a contrary finding, invalidating the ordinance as applied to Allman, noting, "the action by the Board was inconsistent and discriminatory. A discriminatory action is arbitrary and capricious, and bears no reasonable or substantial relation to the public health, safety, morals or general welfare."[23]

The dispute raised in *Board of Supervisors of Fairfax County v. Williams*[24] followed a similar pattern. Here the developer's request for a two tract change from one to almost three units per acre was denied due to highway inadequacy. In supporting the trial court's overruling of the supervisor's position, the Virginia Supreme Court held that:

1. Public facilities did or were soon to be available to serve the land in question.
2. Nearby similarly situated property had already been rezoned for higher density use.
3. The existing zoning on the land was unreasonable and therefore invalid.
4. It was discriminatory and therefore arbitrary and capricious to deny higher density to the land in question.

While these Metropolitan Washington, D.C. counties have attempted to use second generation planning tools to reduce spiraling growth, the court has hindered their efforts. However, the adverse holdings only invalidated the ordinances as applied; their specific rather than general constitutionality was challenged. A case which did address the constitutionality of the plan on its face was Golden v. Ramapo,[25] which some have called the most significant zoning case since *Euclid.*

The Town of Ramapo, located in Rockland County, New York has experienced one of the fastest growth rates in the state due to its proximity to New York City and the opening of the state thruway, the Tappan Zee Bridge, and the Palisades Parkway. At present, Ramapo encompasses 89 square miles covering seven governmental units: the unincorporated area and the six incorporated villages of Sloatsburg, Hillburn, Suffern, Spring Valley, New Square, and Pomona.

Given its location and the present growth rate, it was estimated that by 1979 100,000 people would have fully occupied the town unless steps were taken to preserve the orderly growth of the community. A new master plan was in the process of being developed, but an increase of builders applying to acquire permits under the existing ordinance prompted the passage of an interim development law. With the objective of protecting the integrity of the revised master plan, this interim measure imposed a six-month moratorium on residential building permits in those areas designated for change. In *Rubin v. McAlevey*[26] the court sustained this stop-gap enactment. Later in the year, the master plan was adopted, containing the following key developmental strategies:

1. The population increase provided for in the town's development plan should be kept to a moderate level so that the existing rural, semirural, and suburban character in different parts of the town could be maintained and so that the existing and projected public facilities would not be overburdened.
2. Provisions should be made for adequate public facilities (transportation, circulation, education, recreation) consistent with the anticipated needs of a growing population.
3. The areas of the greatest residential densities should be those in the villages of the town and those closest to the villages. In general, densities should become lower in areas increasingly distant from the village.
4. Residential densities should be consistent with the character and density of surrounding developed areas, topography, the adequacy of circulation and other community facilities and the overall objective of providing for a moderate population increase in the unincorporated portion of the town.[27]

Subsequently, a timing and control ordinance (TASC) was enacted in 1969, culminating a comprehensive planning process that had been continually developed over the years. To provide a tool to carry out these broad policy determinations, the town adopted a six-year capital budget program establishing a firm commitment for the development of the necessary capital improvements in the unincorporated areas.[28] Augmenting this, a twelve-year (two six-year sequences) capital improvement plan was adopted providing a sequencing of infrastructure additions. Integrating the capital plans with the official map, comprehensive plan, and drainage map allowed Ramapo to insure that development proceeded in accordance with stated objectives.

The residential development use permit, added to the town's zoning ordinance, required a residential developer building on unincorporated land to accumulate a total of 15 points from five select categories: public sanitary sewers, drainage facilities, enhanced parks and recreational facilities, improved major secondary and collector roads, and fire houses within appropriate distances. The point system is based on a 0 to 5 scale, with 5 being the best, and is broken down into the following categories:

	Points
Sewers	
Public Sewers available	5
Package Sewer Plants	3
County-approved Septic System	3
All others	0
Drainage (percent capacity available)	
100+	5
98–99.9	4
80–89.9	3
65–79.9	2
50–64.9	1
Less than 50	0
Improved Public Park or Recreational Facility	
Within .25 mile	5
Within .50 mile	3
Within 1 mile	1
Further than 1 mile	0
Improved Roads (state, county, or major town, secondary or collector with curbs and sidewalks)	
Direct Access	5
Within .50 mile	3
Within 1 mile	1
Further than 1 mile	0
Firehouse	
Within 1 mile	3
Within 2 miles	1
Further than 2 miles	0

If the developer anticipates the required amount of points, he usually receives permission to proceed with the project. If not, relief is provided through a variance, reduction of assessed valuation, issuance of development permits at such time as the capital plan indicates facility availability, or if the developer provides the necessary facilities to accumulate the requisite 15 points. More specifically:

1. The builder may advance the authorization date by agreeing to improve facilities, bringing them up to the point requirement. Typically, off-site drainage work or on-site recreational facilities are the types of improvements made.

2. Approval from the town board for an application can be requested if within one year from the date of the application any improvement delineated in the capital budget for completion will bring the point total to 15. Any scheduled improvement in either the capital budget or plan in excess of one year shall be credited as though in existence as of the date of the scheduled completion.

3. The development easement acquisition commission may allow the developer of a site scheduled for development to obtain a reduction on property taxes until the temporary restrictions are taken off the land.

4. Relief can be sought through a variance procedure. If the town board, upon the findings of the planning board, finds that the project is in accordance and reinforces the town's comprehensive planning process, relief from the strict application of the zoning ordinance is provided. Accordingly, a variance for one or two lots is relatively assured, while those greater than this amount are usually denied.

5. A final remedy enables the developer to use the land as authorized under the current ordinance, with the exception of residential uses.

In bringing the Ramapo case, petitioner Golden was denied preliminary subdivision review due to an admitted failure to secure a special permit. The lower court sustained the ordinance, but the appellate division reversed this decision. In turn, New York's highest court reversed this ruling, legitimizing the ordinance, reasoning that "phased growth is well within the ambit of existing enabling legislation."[29]

However, the feasibility of providing services in advance of demand seems a questionable procedure. It would seem that statutory and practical demands placed upon the limited municipal fisc would make such an approach impractical. Justice Breitel mentions this in his Ramapo dissent, indicating that the movement has been in the opposite direction, first the demand, then services commensurate with this need.[30] Richard Babcock succinctly summarizes this, noting:

> The economic and social mobility and the growth of American society is attributable in large part to the frontier psychology which insisted that the availability of public services follows the demand rather than controls it. Without this premise, we would have never crossed the Alleghenies.[31]

The New York enabling statute authorizes a six-year capital program; however, Ramapo's CIP represented three successive six-year programs. Though Golden argued that the second and third stages would bind the hands of future legislators, the court did not concur, seeing no reason to assume that the town would renege on its plan. However, as outlined later, the town, though not purposefully, has been unable to keep to the schedule.

The reason for advancing service provisions ahead of development is to enable the municipality to make decisions regarding expansion, rather than simply responding to development pressures. However, the conception that the developer is solely profit-oriented and the planning board is solely acting for the public good is a spurious notion which assumes that overcrowding, blight, and all attendant adverse impacts are the product of a laissez-faire land use system which commits the allocation of land resources at the developer's will. It allows localities to exonerate themselves from their own poor planning and, returning to the notion of how development actually occurs, for their own short-sighted decisions. While the developer may initiate the planning review process, private sector building is in response to a perceived demand, a penetrable market. Petaluma affords a case in point. Despite the town's mandate to equalize housing disparity within its eastern and western sectors, only 59 out of 130 permissible units were bid for in the western, multifamily category—less than half of the allowable units allotted.

Assuming there have been no unfavorable court decisions upholding the developer's point of view, local officials have the final say as to what gets approved. "There are those who claim the urban development process is chaotic: that it is ruled by the random whims of profit-seeking developers whose actions are neither systematic nor predictable. The gross error of such a perception can be particularly pernicious if it is held by those in a position to influence urban plans and policy. The urban development process is a reasonably predictable, systematic interaction of a describable and finite set of relationships."[32]

Assuming that service extension prior to development is realistic, another fault of these controls is their exclusive nature. In Ramapo, as in Fairfax, Montgomery, and Prince Georges counties, the adequate facilities plan was superimposed over an already restrictive program. Not only were minimum lot and subdivision requirements stringent, but the developer was required to first secure permission based on the plan's proximity to existing capacities to apply for zoning, subdivision, and building code approval. Prior to Ramapo's TASC enactment, multifamily housing, on a magnitude of eight to ten dwelling units per acre, was allowed. Under the plan, the lots ranged from 7,500 to 80,000 square-feet (43,560 equaling 1 acre), but only 1 percent of the vacant land was zoned for the lower allowance, with 65 percent falling in the 25,000 to 80,000 classification. Similarly, the low-income housing Ramapo boasts about consists of 200 multifamily units. Out of these, most are occupied by an elderly white population, with only 10 percent of the forty-nine low- and moderate-income dwellings having black occupants.[33]

The Ramapo effort seeks to control only residential development, nonresidential uses are ignored. While the extent of the job and home match is the subject of much speculation, with little empirical evidence, it seems amiss to control an individual's home but not his or her work place:

It is easy to confuse causes and effects in urban growth. Most such growth is caused by an initial economic impulse that brings about increases in the number of jobs. These job increases in turn bring population into an area, and the increased population needs more residences. Thus, trying to control growth by controlling residential works on effects after the causes have occurred.[34]

Some of the systems that have established a quantitative scale, such as Ramapo and the Metropolitan Washington, D.C. counties, impose these controls on an across the board basis, without any allowance made for physiographic differences. Furthermore, the point ranking system and service criteria in these systems are arbitrary and do not relate to any urgent health or safety matters. Under the Ramapo plan, roads must have sidewalks and curbs to receive points. This seems highly unreasonable in light of the fact that the county and state roads in the township are without them. The requirement that there be septic tanks on 2-acre parcels is not supported by any health emergency finding, and is more restrictive than the county health department's standards. Similarly, recreational specifications are overstated in view of the fact that practically 30 percent of the town's total acreage is devoted to parks and recreation. Regarding the merits of Fairfax's low-cost housing bonus, the scaling system gives more credence to best sewer, drainage, or park availability (five points), than to a developer who provides 30 percent low- to moderate-income housing (four points). Providing a quarter of the units to low-income segments is ranked equally with fire house and police station proximity. Furthermore, the problem with access as a measurement is that it says nothing about capacity. The presence of a fire house, police station, or a road within specified distances does not assure that these facilities can adequately service the proposed development. If capacity delineations are to continue, they need to be based upon some performance standards versus arbitrary access approximations.

A more substantive criticism concerns a CIP's ability to accord services based on its timetable. Ramapo has proven disastrous in this regard. Of the thirty-seven projects scheduled for the 1969-1974 period, less than half have been completed. Of the four items scheduled for 1975, only one has materialized. Three of the four 1976 projects have been carried forward from previous years.[35] While Ramapo is still in its infancy in regard to its eighteen-year undertaking, it has already deviated from initial intentions. The relief provisions in the Fairfax and Ramapo plans—which permit the developer to advance a vested interest in property in that year in which provisions are programmed, regardless of their actual existence—are legally expeditious, but antithetical to the planning program. They reduce the burden placed on the developer but thwart equalization of service and demand objectives. If the CIP cannot be adhered to, developers will have a vested right to build regardless of proximity to existing services and, thus, violate the very motivation of the plan. Compounding this is the uncertainty of future CIP allocations due to the public's decision to pass bonds to fund these undertakings, and one legislature's inability to bind the hands of future legislatures. If capital is not supplied commensurate with the programmed services, the plan's backbone and continuity are destroyed.

In Ramapo, the delineation of the capital programs amounted to three fact sheets, simply listing proposed improvements and their estimated costs. Though the Ramapo scheme was anchored to an exhaustive planning process, "taken by themselves, these lists do not provide an impressive backstop for the majority opinion."[36] As Norman Williams pointed out, the entire Ramapo scheme would have a much stronger basis, both substantively and legally, if it had been carried out to its logical conclusion: that is, if one of the final products of the entire scheme had been a map indicating which areas were planned to be developed, with public facilities and with housing, in which years, so that the town could really see and evaluate the proposed growth pattern, and each landowner could tell more or less when his turn would come.[37]

Aside from the previously discussed flaws in the Ramapo plan, the most serious impediment to a viable phasing program is the conditioning of development to services outside the municipality's control. Conditioning development to water and sewer standards is unrealistic for both are set for regional agencies, according to regional needs and demands. How can a developer be denied permission to build due to water and sewer insufficiencies, when the agency does not even have the power to rectify the situation?

Regarding Ramapo's deviation from the CIP, the fact is that the town relies on Rockland County's construction program. Township upstream drainage additions are contingent upon the county's downstream progress. The town does not have any control over firehouses, and drainage programs are under the county's control. Therefore, the CIP and the point system has not facilitated a systematic timing and sequencing program.

In examining other plans' program deficiencies, San Jose illustrates another problem. Four factors contributed to the schools' overcrowding: inadequate planning, voter disapproval of bond issues, political-legal restraints preventing optimum use of available school space, and dependency on state money for school construction.[38] Nevertheless, developers are penalized due to municipal shortcomings and exogenous factors.

Despite the fact that tentative findings have discerned minimal impacts on residential construction, developers are forced into a highly inequitable situation. More basic, this new attitude represents a shift in the method of who pays for what services. Traditionally, the municipality has provided the necessary facilities by floating bonds. However, as in Milford, rapid suburbanization has pushed bonding limits to their ceilings in San Jose. The salient point is that this expansion produces a sudden increase from one level of public expenditure to a higher level, rather than a uniform increase. Fiscal and institutional restraints on borrowing capabilities make it difficult to accommodate this concentration of expenditure within a short time. Circumventing this, localities have adopted marginal pricing policies, making newcomers, and not all residents as a whole, bear the cost of increased services. Twenty years ago, Philip Green remarked that, "maybe the problem of keeping abreast of development is essentially one of local government finance, with the solution not holding development, but revamping the structure of local government finance."[39]

While exactions are permissible within certain parameters, the problem is that a developer gets penalized, not for the content of the proposal, but for the time at which he comes in. He pays for unfortunate timing—coming in when services are approaching the saturation level. An additional regressive aspect is that the extra costs imposed are financed at construction loan rates (10 to 12 percent), considerably higher than what the locality can float bonds at (5 to 7 percent). This is usually not absorbed by the developer but passed on to the homebuyer, increasing housing costs.

In determining who should be responsible for the services upon which development is conditioned, the Advisory Commission on Intergovernmental Relations has suggested the following standards:

1. The governmental jurisdiction responsible for providing the service should be large enough for the benefits from that service to be received primarily by its own population.
2. The unit of government should be large enough to permit economies of scale.
3. The agency carrying on this function should have control over a geographic area which, in terms of scale and physiographic features, allows for effective performance.
4. The unit of government should have the legal-financial-administrative ability to perform services assigned to it.[40]

Returning to another objective of adequate facility regulations, the controls are designed to reduce sprawl. But if the controls are to be effective, it is important to distinguish what type of sprawl. Harvey and Clark have posited three types: low density—continuous developments containing large lots; ribbon development—segments compact within themselves, strung out along highways, with intervening areas undeveloped; leap-frog development—a collection of discontinuous urban pockets.[41]

Each of these types of development produces different effects on the cost of urban services. Programs such as the Metropolitan Washington, D.C. counties or Ramapo do not counter sprawl, but rather encourage and program it. Present trends are merely slowed down over time without innovative, planned development provisions. Consequently, sprawl will continue; the pattern of growth will approximate the past but at a reduced rate. Furthermore, basing the capital improvement program on reduced services provisions "locks" the municipality into low-intensity development. Cluster or planned development flexibility is destroyed because the infrastructure extensions are geared to low-density uses. Central program elements—reducing sprawl and affording flexible control mechanisms—are lost: "So conceived, city planning is little more than the translation of basic principles of civil engineering into suggested guidelines for development that minimize the cost of public facilities."[42]

Since zoning's legitimization fifty years ago, planning has continuously tested new frontiers regarding private property rights against governmental regulations. The advent of APF programming raises additional questions. To what extent does the municipality have to provide services to its population, and how hard must it try to do so? These questions along with equal protection, due process, and fundamental rights doctrines will be the focus of the next section.

NOTES

1. American Society of Planning Officials, "Clinic: Development Timing," *Planning 1955* (Chicago: American Society of Planning Officials, 1956), p. 88.
2. Matter of Josephs v. Town Board of Clarkstown 198 N.Y.S. 2d 695 (1960).
3. Norman Williams, *American Land Planning Law,* Vol. III (Chicago; Callaghan and Company, 1976), p. 357.
4. *Ibid.*
5. Christopher Bell, "Controlling Residential Development on the Urban Fringe: St. Louis, Missouri," 48 *Journal of Urban Law* 409 (1971).
6. Gleeson, et al., "Urban Growth Management Systems," *Planning Advisory Service,* Report Numbers 309, 310 (Chicago: American Society of Planning Officials, 1975), p. 12.
7. *Ibid.,* p. 21.
8. "Land Use Growth Controls: A Case Study of San Jose and Livermore, California," 15 *Santa Clara Lawyer* 1, 22 (1974).
9. Gleeson, "Urban Growth," p. 19.
10. *History and Evaluation of the 1971-1972 Local Government Structure Study,* Milpitas Planning Department, Milpitas, California, 1972.
11. "Land Use Growth Controls," p. 8.
12. Builders Association of Santa Clara — Cruz Counties v City of San Jose. Docket number 293759, California Superior Court, November 23, 1973.
13. Michael D. White, "Water as a Tool in Land Use Control, Legal Considerations: An Exploratory Essay," 20 *Rocky Mountain Mineral Law Institute* 671, 673 (1975).
14. Donald Downing, *The Role of Water and Sewer Extension Financing in Guiding Urban Residential Growth,* Report Number 19, Water Resources Research Center, University of Tennessee, 1972, p. 6.
15. A solid description of this program is found in: "Capital Improvement Programming — Some Considerations," *Planning Advisory Service,* Report Number 23 (Chicago: American Society of Planning Officials, 1951).
16. Gleeson, "Urban Growth," p. 6.

17. Maryland National Capital Park and Planning Commission v. Rosenberg 307 A. 2d 704, 706 (1973).
18. Beane v. Maryland National Capital Park and Planning Commission. Docket Number 56-864, Circuit Court of Prince Georges County, 1974.
19. *Montgomery County Adequate Public Facilities Ordinance,* Montgomery County, Maryland, Ordinance Number 7-41, 1972, pp. 2 and 3.
20. Donald Downing, *Pricing and Investment Policy for Sewer Extensions: A Potential Growth Control Tool for Montgomery County, Maryland,* submitted at the American Institute of Planners 1974 Confer-In, Paper Number 205, 1974, p. 5.
21. Robert Freilich, *The Legal Basis for a Growth Control System in Fairfax County, Virginia,* PLUS Program Research Paper 2, submitted to the Board of Supervisors of Fairfax County, 1973, p. 72.
22. Docket Numbers 730991 and 740029, Circuit Court of Fairfax County, January 20, 1975.
23. *Ibid* at 15.
24. Docket Numbers 730996, Virginia Supreme Court, July, 1975.
25. In an American Society of Planning Officials polling of leading planning law professors, their response showed that Ramapo was the most significant case since the validity of zoning in Euclid. See: *Planning Magazine* 8/6 (Chicago: American Society of Planning Officials, 1972), pp. 108, 109.
26. 288 N.Y.S. 2d 519 (1968).
27. Manuel Emanuel, "Ramapo's Managed Growth Program: A Close look at Ramapo After Five Years Experience," *Planners Notebook,* 4/5 (Washington, D.C.: American Institute of Planners, 1974), p. 2.
28. The reason for this and the subsequent application of controls to only the unincorporated areas is that they are within the town's jurisdiction, although they lie within the town boundaries.
29. 285 N.E.2d 291, 300 (1972).
30. *Ibid* at 310.
31. Richard Babcock, *The Zoning Game – Municipal Practices and Policies* (Madison, Wisconsin: University of Wisconsin Press, 1969), p. 149.
32. Claude Gruen, "The Economics of Petaluma: Unconstitutional Regional Socio-Economic Impacts," in *Management and Control of Growth,* Vol. II, edited by R. Scott (Washington, D.C.: The Urban Land Institute, 1975), p. 175.
33. Herbert Franklin, *Controlling Urban Growth – But for Whom?* (Washington, D.C.: Potomac Institute, Inc., Metropolitan Housing Program, 1973), pp. 14 and 38 (at footnote 15).
34. Robert Levine, *Growth Control: Some Questions For Urban Decision Makers,* prepared for The National Science Foundation, Washington, D.C., Number R-1419, 1974, p. 2.
35. *Report On The National Association of Home Builders' Task Force Field Trip to Ramapo, New York,* National Association of Home Builders, Washington, D.C., May, 1975, p. 10.
36. Williams, *American Land,* p. 370.
37. *Ibid.*
38. *Evaluation of the Effects of Measure B,* Working Paper Number 1, A Consultants Report for the Measure B Study, April, 1975, p. 8.
39. American Society of Planning Officials, "Clinic: Development Timing," p. 56.

40. Advisory Commission on Intergovernmental Relations, *Metropolitan America: Challenge to Federalism* (Washington, D.C.: Government Printing Office, 1960), pp. 30-32.
41. Harvey and Clark, "Controlling Urban Growth: The New Zealand and Australian Experiment," 32 *Appraisal Journal* 551 (1964).
42. Fred Bosselman, "Can the Town of Ramapo Pass A Law To Bind the Rights of the Whole World?" 1 *Florida State University Law Review.* 234, 244 (1974).

Chapter Ten:
Legal Considerations

The conflict arising between a landowner's property rights and societal impositions on these rights raises many legal questions. Jurisdictions charting a growth management program find their legitimacy established within constitutional limitations on government regulation of private actions. Within such a construct, plans are typically evaluated legally in regard to the following legal doctrines: due process, equal protection, and fundamental rights.

First, the court looks at the reasonableness of the mechanism. Absent a clear-cut legal infringement, the presumption of validity is attached to the municipality's plan, validating it unless proved otherwise. However, in the last few years there have been departures from this legislative deference—where the judiciary more often looks to the intent and application of the plan. For example, regional plans which do not take physiographic features into account will no longer be validated, nor plans which abridge fundamental rights or are exclusionary on the basis of race, sex, and so forth. Absent compelling state interests to justify the imposition, the management plan will be voided.

While this more enlightened view is welcomed it is important to remember that it is the job of the courts to make sure the planner does his job but not do it for him.

Usually, courts first attempt to discern the reasonableness of the regulations which support the plan. In assessing this criterion, the court typically balances the plan's purported goals and objectives against the legitimacy of the regulatory powers utilized. More refined, an evaluative framework determines whether:

1. The regulation promotes a proper objective within the governmental concern, and if there is a clear relationship between the regulation and the objective;
2. Landowners similarly situated receive equal treatment;
3. The objective produces a benefit to the entire community for which compensation must be paid;
4. The regulations do not diminish the property value too severely.[1]

Judicial review determines whether the regulation is encompassed within the ambit of the "police power"—promoting the public health, safety, and welfare. Legislative deference, or the presumption of an ordinance's validity, is usually applied, upholding a measure unless the plaintiff can prove that the involved officials acted in an "arbitrary" or "capricious" fashion, ignoring public objectives permitted under statutory of unconstitutional law. The role of the judiciary in reviewing zoning ordinances adopted pursuant to the statutory grant of power is narrow. The court may act only if the presumption in favor of the validity of the ordinance is overcome by a showing that it is unreasonable or arbitrary. However, a more strict judicial review may be triggered if it can be shown that governmental enactments impinge upon "fundamental rights" or "suspect classifications," which result in exclusionary effects. Virtually all regulations impose restrictions; however, the judiciary regards exclusion as a purposeful attempt, either expressed or in effect, to isolate certain classes of people. In expanded versions of the exclusionary argument, regulations have been challenged on grounds that they violated the "right to travel." This doctrine does not assert explicit discrimination per se, but rather contends that mechanisms burdening an individual's rights to free mobility are inherently illegal.

A frequent allegation against growth limiting plans is that they place "undue and harsh" burdens on an individual's property and are "confiscatory," taking land without just compensation. Another area of legal concern addresses the unauthorized exercise of the town's zoning power. The court determines whether the agency implementing the plan is empowered to do so and has not exceeded its authority under the state enabling legislation.

In sum, all of the latter arguments evolve from the legal doctrines of due process, equal protection, and state enabling authority. We will now examine these in light of present case law and planning practices.

Since the *Euclid*[2] decision, communities have regulated and divided their territorial areas into conventional and, more recently, planned development districts. However, a narrow reading of statutory powers has disallowed ordinances which regulate the timing of development, considering such ordinances as taking of land without just compensation. Consequently, communities have used zoning devices to control the sequence of development. Holding zones, minimum lot and floor restrictions, exclusion of multifamily configurations, and other devices have all been used for this purpose. Because the courts have traditionally deferred to legislative action, communities have been able to promulgate such regulations and hide behind a "judicial shield," knowing the developer must overcome a formidable burden of proof.

In making a due process determination, the court typically investigates the legitimacy of the exposed objectives and whether the means employed to achieve such objectives are within the scope of the police power. Usually, this decision is not based on any in-depth analysis. Upon finding that the regulations are within the ambit of the police power, the reasonableness of the action is then scrutinized.

Actions brought can challenge general or specific constitutional grounds. In the latter case, allegations usually encompass unreasonable planning board actions or a taking of land without just compensation. Prior to Justice Holmes' admonition in *Pennsylvania Coal Co. v. Mahon,*[3] the police power was held not to be circumscribed by the taking clause in the Fifth Amendment but only by the reasonableness requirement of the Fourteenth Amendment. Despite this expansion, the developer's burden was still difficult, compounded by the fact that legislative bodies are oftentimes not required to provide justifications for their actions, and if they do, records maintained are sketchy and incomplete. However, judicial attitude is changing in some state courts, prompting a more refined review of this matter. The judiciary is looking beyond superficial delineations of purposes and means, scrutinizing the real intent of the municipality's regulations. The controlling determination is whether the community is realistically attempting to accommodate growth or merely constructing exclusionary walls.

In making this determination, several courts have discarded the presumption of a zoning ordinance's validity, to get to the substantive issues, when:

1. The plaintiff is able to show that the community has totally excluded a use that is not a nuisance.
2. Certain uses are given a preferred status and as such may not be disallowed unless there is some compelling state purpose.
3. The zoning decision made is administrative in nature.[4]

The first scenario has been applied in the so-called Pennsylvania and New Jersey cases. Examining the plan from a regional perspective, the court scrutinized the locality's obligation to accommodate a variety of income strata. Finding large-lot unconstitutional, the *Kit-Mar*[5] and *National Land*[6] cases express the court's discontent with municipal regulations which "stand in the

way of the natural forces which send our growing population into hitherto
undeveloped areas in search of a comfortable place to live."[7] The *Mt. Laurel*,[8]
Girsh,[9] and *Chesterdale Farms*[10] cases represent that the denial of multifamily
configurations violates the due process clause of the Constitution, depriving
lower income groups of adequate housing.[11]

An argument over "preferred status" was the basis of a Michigan case,
Bristow v. City of Woodhaven.[12] In limiting the amount of mobile homes
permitted in trailer parks, the court interpreted the general welfare interest to be
considered in light of general community needs. Thus, the court found that
certain uses, mobile homes being one of them, are afforded a preferred status;
dissolving the presumption of validity, the court shifted the burden to the
muicipality to justify its exclusion.

In *Fasano v. Board of County Commissioners of Washington County*[13] the
court held that zoning amendments which affect specific projects or parcels are
treated as administrative actions. In making such a determination, due process
deficiencies previously alluded to are overcome, compelling the municipality to
undertake a full-scale hearing, allowing cross-examination, establishing findings
of fact, and producing, and justifying, the board's action. While this substantially
enlarges the scope of review on appeal, the *Fasano* case reinforces growth
management programs by making it harder for developers seeking zoning
changes to secure them. In the words of the court, "the burden of proof should
be placed, as is usual in judicial proceedings, upon the one seeking the change.
The more drastic the change, the greater will be the burden of showing that it is
in conformance with the comprehensive plan as implemented by the ordinance,
that there is a public need for the kind of change in question, and that the need
is best met by the proposal under consideration."[14]

Forcing the governing body to establish a written record and to justify its
findings is superior to current practices because the board's conclusions would
no longer be hidden and could be debated on their merits. Furthermore, findings
can be weighed against established criteria in making a determination of
reasonableness. Without such an articulation, project denials promulgated on
seemingly legitimate purposes could be mere veils for illicit and invidious
actions.[15]

The main difficulty lies in defining what types of actions trigger active
judicial intervention. Under the "old" equal protection doctrine, the
classification must be proven unreasonable and arbitrary. The deficiencies with
this approach have been previously described. A more liberal interpretation calls
for stricter circumspection when the governmental action infringes upon an
individual's right or is an arbitrary or unreasonable classification.[16] Courts are
less patient when fundamental rights are abridged or suspect classifications
created.

In making this transition the reasoning has been that presumed rationality
does not significantly deter municipal overregulation and, therefore, the

judiciary needs to be able to scrutinize such excesses. If a guarded right is impinged, the state must then show the regulation is within its police powers, achieving a compelling state interest, and the rule is narrowly drawn. Specifically, the test encompasses: a determination if the law establishes a classification; if the compelling interest proferred by the state is substantial enough to warrant such imposition; and a finding of less imposing alternatives.[17]

The district court opinion in the *Petaluma* case offers a prime example of this process. *Construction Industry Association of Sonoma County v. City of Petaluma*[18] marked the first time the fundamental right to travel doctrine was employed against land use controls. In attempting to evoke stricter judicial review, the plaintiff contended that the numerical quota in the city's plan subverted the constitutionally guaranteed right of travel. To counter this contention, the city posited three compelling state interests:

1. The sewage treatment facilities were inadequate to absorb uncontrolled growth.
2. The water capacity was finite and unable to support a large population.
3. That zoning powers enable the city to control its own rate of growth and to protect the community's character.

After evaluating the merit of the governmental rebuttal, the court found that the sewage facilities were capable of being expanded to meet projected population increases, the city purposefully limited its water supply contract, and that an agency capable of accommodating resident growth may not avoid doing so simply because it prefers not to expand at the market rate. The fact that the compelling interest test was not upheld prompted Judge Burke to comment that, "the city is able, at the present time, to return to absorption of existing market and demographic growth rates without exceeding the capacity of city facilities."[19]

Relying on doctrines evolving from the series of Pennsylvania cases previously mentioned, the court announced that Petaluma could not ignore its surrounding areas and must be responsive to current market demand and demographic trends: "Since the population limitation policies complained of are not supported by a compelling governmental interest, the exclusionary aspects of the Petaluma Plan must be, and are hereby declared in violation of the right to travel and hence, are unconstitutional."[20] After reaching this conclusion, objections under the commerce clause and remaining equal protection arguments were dismissed.

Relying on the right to travel, the court cited cases which primarily used this doctrine in limiting durational residency requirements. *Shapiro v. Thompson*[21] and its progeny[22] have found the fundamental travel right burdened when municipalities impose any type of tenure mandates to voting, welfare public housing, and medical privileges. By applying this right to land use regulations, the court in the Petaluma case avoided the dicta in *Lindsey v. Normant.*[23] In *Lindsey* month-to-month tenants refused to pay their rent unless certain violations of the building code were remedied. In refusing to apply the newer equal protection, the court rejected the plaintiff's contention that the need for decent shelter and the right to retain peaceful possession of one's home constitutes a fundamental interest. Though the court goes on record stating the importance of decent, safe, and sanitary housing, they conclude that absent a constitutional mandate, housing is a legislative not a judicial function.[24] This prompted one writer to criticize the court's holding, reasoning that a constitutional right to housing is a necessary complement to the initiative already demonstrated by the legislative and executive branches.[25]

Even if the court subscribed to a fundamental right of housing, its constitutional source raises other problems. Relying upon the right to migrate and settle as a fundamental liberty would seemingly extend the right to travel to both interstate and intrastate movement. On the other hand, if the fundamental nature of this right was restricted to an equal protection context, strict scrutiny would be triggered only when an individual's right of travel was infringed upon in a discriminatory manner. In applying this doctrine, the Supreme Court has historically viewed travel almost exclusively in terms of interstate mobility. As such, local land use regulations barring intrastate movement circumvent the travel argument. *Memorial Hospital v. Maricopa County*[26] lends credence to this view. Even though the imposed one-year residency stipulation for free nonemergency medical indigent care penalized both intrastate and interstate travelers, Justice Marshall restricted his opinion to interstate considerations, avoiding the Arizona's court's construction that the requirement was equally applicable to both situations.[27] However, starting with *Shapiro,* and reinforced by two circuit court opinions, a precedent for the personal right to travel is evolving. The first circuit court's invalidation of Rhode Island residency requirements for public housing failed to distinguish between the intrastate and interstate residents.[28] This was carried further in *King v. New Rochelle Municipal Housing Authority,* in which the court averred that "it would be meaningless to describe the right to travel between states as a fundamental precept of personal liberty and not to acknowledge a correlative constitutional right to travel within a state."[29] However, if there arises a tendency to apply the right to travel doctrine to intrastate mobility, land use regulations would be jeopardized with "few land use regulations likely to survive in their present form."[30]

However, to apply the durational residency tests set by the court to land use regulations is misdirected. Land use ordinances cut across many boundaries and are not readily susceptible to the same analysis. Land use regulations do not only affect those individuals who wish to migrate; they affect all present and prospective residents of the area. Furthermore, specific privileges or benefits are not singled out, but imposed in varying degrees on a variety of private interests.

This has led some to propose alternative review measures which would impose a "heightened rationality" test.[31] The emerging synthesis narrows the fundamental right requirements while expanding judicial scrutiny of the safeguarding of these rights. Basically, this is the type of review afforded in the New Jersey and Pennsylvania cases. Ordinances withstanding constitutional objections are then examined, taking into account regional growth patterns. As such, interests of future residents are protected but not at the expense of the locality's ability to plan. Additionally, "this course of action would provide textural framework for future adjudication concerning the right to travel and would avoid a potential problem suggested by *Petaluma*—that if landowners should be denied standing to assert the travel right of potential residents, the outcome of litigation challenging the land use ordinance might be dependent upon the identity of the plaintiff."[32]

The problem is that few courts are willing to meet this challenge. The salient criticism of this test is that it is beyond the scope of judicial power. In usurping legislative power, the judiciary is making subjective evaluations rather than deciding the issues on the basis of legal doctrines. This philosophy is illustrated in the ninth circuit court's disposition of the *Petaluma* appeal. After decreeing that the construction industry did not have standing to assert the right to travel for third parties, the court summarily dismissed the substantive due process charge noting that, "being neither a super legislative nor a zoning board of appeal, a federal court is without authority to weigh and reappraise the facts considered or ignored by the legislative body in passing the challenged zoning regulation."[33] In fact, the accompanying footnote asserts the court's apparent anger at the appellee's brief for its longevity, filled with planning, economic, and sociological themes: "These types of considerations are more appropriate for legislative bodies then for courts."[34]

Petaluma raises another question—namely, who is entitled standing to bring such actions? Traditionally, the stated purpose of standing was to allow only those specifically, personally, and adversely aggrieved to bring suit. Initially this meant only property owners. However, a broader interpretation allows individuals to bring suit if they: allege that the action challenged has caused them injury in fact; and show that the interest asserted is within the zone of interests sought to be protected or regulated by the statute or constitutional guarantee in question.[35]

Basically this means that in addition to proving a sufficiently personal stake in the outcome, the relief sought must be within the judiciary's power to grant, assuming this will not infringe upon legislative territory. In subjecting the *Petaluma* challenge to this two-tiered analysis, Judge Choy acknowledges that the construction industry easily satisfies the "injury in fact standing requirements." However, the industry failed on the second test, the "zone of interest" requirement.[36] The right to travel assertion was made on behalf of unknown third parties so "their economic interests are undisputedly outside the zone of interest to be protected by any purported constitutional right to travel."[37] This same stumbling block was evident in the recent *Warth v. Seldin* case.[38] Claiming Penfield, New York's zoning ordinance effectively excluded low- and moderate-income groups from living in the town, various nonresidents, organizations, and residents alleged a violation of their rights, privileges, and immunities secured by the Constitution and the laws of the United States. To relieve these harms the petitioners asked the court to declare the ordinance unconstitutional, to enjoin the defendants from enforcing the ordinance, to order a new ordinance designed to remedy this situation, and to award $750,000 in actual and exemplary damages.

In making the threshold determination whether to entertain the suit, the court found injury and fact indicating a motion to dismiss. As in *Petaluma,* the requisite relief condition was not met. In other words, the court did not see how granting the requested relief would improve the plaintiff's position. Because none of the petitioners were on the threshold of development, an invalidation of Penfield's ordinance would not bring about any new housing. While this reasoning is logical, when *Warth* is combined with *Petaluma* (not granting standing to either the construction industry or nonresidents) one wonders how exclusionary zoning suits can be brought in the federal courts. In attempting to distinguish *Warth, Petaluma's* petition for a rehearing *en banc* claims that the Ninth Circuit misread *Warth's* language by suggesting that the plaintiff cannot rest his claim for relief on the legal rights or interests of third parties. This controverts the court's declaration in the *Warth* case "of the right to assert the interests of third persons when the plaintiff has made out injury in fact to himself."[39] Not swayed by such a position, the ninth circuit court denied a rehearing, with the construction industry appealing to the Supreme Court. The Supreme Court denied *certiorari,* thus finally legitimizing the plan.

These recent situations make practitioners question the proper forum for such actions. The fact that the federal courts have practically abandoned zoning challenges since the mid-1920s prompted Richard Babcock to note that, "it is an enormous if not fatal error for opponents of exclusionary zoning to bring these cases in the deferal courts . . .; the federal courts feel obliged to base their decisions on racial, not economic discrimination."[40] Exemplary of this attitude are the decisions compelling municipalities to provide services upon a finding that extension denials were racially motivated. *Hawkins v. Shaw*[41] is a leading case, mandating equalization of service provisions to black and white neighborhoods. Alleging discriminatory provisions of varied municipal services, black citizens of Shaw, Mississippi sought injunctive relief. Using a variety of statistical evidence, the plaintiffs established a *prima facie* case of racial discrimination in service levels accorded white and black residents. Contrary to the lower court's more permissive "rational basis standard," the fifth circuit court found a suspect classification, triggering stricter scrutiny. This more rigorous review compelled the town to justify the service disparity to sustain its actions. Traffic impacts, spatial proximity, and intensity of use justifications proferred by the town were found to be insufficient to overcome the burden of proof. Subsequently, the court deemed that the unequal treatment of different racial neighborhoods violates the equal protection clause of the Fourteenth Amendment.[42]

Absent invidious classifications, *Shaw* left untouched the situation of mandatory facility expansion to meet some level of anticipated demand. In light of the numerous adequate facility ordinances, it is this less precise area that we will now attempt to examine.

Originating under common law, and incorporated with state statutes, it is usually assumed by the judiciary that utilities possess ample authority to provide services, issue bonds, and exercise control over their functioning. Reasons justifying this: consider the allocation of finite resources; view citizen voting power a sufficient deterrent to excessive discretion; reflect that enlightened public administration requires flexibility to apply innovative techniques; and avoid forced governmental participation in the success of prospective development.[43]

An early illustration of the court's interpretation of public facilities ordinances surfaced sixty-three years ago in Maine. When an individual was refused utility extension based on the utility's determination not to raise rates or issue bonds, the denied individual sued. Dismissing the petitioner's allegation "that the district need supply all within its jurisdiction," Maine's Supreme Judicial Court upheld the trustees' refusal to extend, reasoning that the state legislature had intended the trustees to exercise such discretion, even without any explicit mandate to do so.[44]

An obligation exists to offer services only as far as the utility's undertaking. However, once this threshold is passed, the utility cannot retrack from providing services to all within its service area in a nondiscriminatory fashion. This represents a generalized notion that when a municipality secures an exclusive franchise in an area, or it provides services similar to those offered by others, the utility becomes a public entity, and is required to serve all customers to the extent of its capacity. A qualification on this "transition" takes into account the magnitude of public demand, the expense of the operation, revenues and other business considerations.[45]

An example of the latter occurred in Boulder, Colorado. Establishing a policy of ordering fringe development, water and sewer extensions outside the city's jurisdictional limits were permitted only under strict review. When a proposal deemed incompatible with the city's growth policies was denied, the landowner instituted court proceedings. Finding that Boulder secured total control over all infrastructure provisions in this area, the court likened the city's operation to that of a public utility which is to provide nondiscriminatory servicing. The fact that two other proximate sites had water and sewer lines and system capacity existed obligated the city to furnish such facilities.[46] A different set of challenges arose to the adequate facilities ordinances (APF) promulgated in the Washington Metropolitan Area counties.

The Prince Georges County APF discussed in the previous section was challenged when petitioner Rosenberg's preliminary subdivision approval was denied. The county had denied approval because the application was not backed with adequate facilities. Revised testimony that there was actually a 251 surplus school capacity prompted the court to view the planning board's refusal as arbitrary and capricious.[47] An initial problem, which became mute, was that under the capital improvement program no additions were planned to the schools in this vicinity; essentially this policy was a permanent injunction against all development. Norman Williams, the legal architect of the previously discussed Clarkstown plan, commented that a major reason for the legitimization of the scheme was that the Clarkstown central school district was in fact proceeding to build schools on a regular schedule. The opinion noted "everything reasonably possible is being done by the local authorities to meet the urgency in the school situation."[48] It seems likely that this served as the salient legal bulwark of the validity of the whole scheme. To be effective, the arbitrary nature of these actions cannot be tolerated.

The *Rosenberg* decision was relied upon in a similar challenge to Prince Georges' adequate facilities plan. *In Beane v. Maryland National Capital Park and Planning Commission*,[49] the confrontation arose from the board's denial of Beane's preliminary plan approval. This refusal was premised on the inability of the transportation network to accommodate all the traffic generated from the site. Unlike *Rosenberg,* the capital improvement program had scheduled improvements to these routes within six years. In dismissing the plaintiff's contention of a "taking," the judiciary found that he was currently using his land pursuant to a permitted use. Subsequently, the scope of judicial review was narrowed to the unreasonableness of the board's decision. Despite the apparent rationality in the board's determination, the court found that the site in question had three alternative access points, two of which were adequate to handle all traffic any hour of the day. Seemingly, the board's rejection was premised on the inadequacy of only one of these access points, disregarding the other two. As a result, the court found the plan unconstitutional as applied.[50]

Indicative of the opinions in the Prince Georges County case, neighboring Fairfax County was unable to sustain two specific constitutional charges against its adequate facilities ordinance. In the first case,[51] the plaintiff's rezoning request—from one to three units per acre—was denied. Remanding this case, the court asked the board to reconsider its actions. Upon the board's failure to reonsider the remand, the trial court ordered the subject's property zoned to the requested PDH-3 district.[52] While justifiably angered by the board's inertia, the trial court's decision represents a clear case of excessive judicial power. The court violated the separation of powers doctrine by legislating for the legislature. Upon review, the circuit court admonished that the court may not rezone property to specific categories upon a finding of the invalidity of a zoning ordinance.[53]

A similar but less excessive procedure is found in Pennsylvania. Section 1011 of the Municipal Planning Code enables the court to approve the specific plan, in part or in its entirety, upon a finding that the local restrictions unlawfully prevent or restrict a development or use. Not only can the judiciary invalidate a local provision, it is also empowered to direct the municipality to build the project litigated. As such, it adds teeth to successful exclusionary zoning challenges which only result in invalidating exclusionary zoning, but do nothing to encourage development. Obviously, if judicial review of local zoning action is to result in anything more than a farce, the courts must be prepared to go beyond mere invalidation and grant "definitive relief."[54]

However, caution would have to be exercised in such a mandate for the possibility exists of judicial circumvention of comprehensive planning. Litigation typically arises in the zoning stage. However, a finding in the developer's favor only allows him to then proceed for subdivision and building code review. Definitive relief in the form of a court order giving a developer a project, without requiring subdivision and building code review, is antithetical to the planning process. Subsequent Pennsylvania case law addresses this issue. In *Casey v. Zoning and Hearing Board of Warwick Township*[55] the landowner brought suit attacking the constitutionality of the zoning ordinance. The court of common pleas affirmed the landowner's challenge, but refused to order building permit approval. On appeal, the commonwealth court directed the requisite permits granted. Upon final disposition, the Pennsylvania Supreme Court held that in a case in which the proposed development had made no demands upon the appropriate agencies for nonzoning considerations, "we cannot say that the appellee is entitled to the building permit, as a matter of right . . . . He must satisfy the requirements of the other sources of control (i.e., subdivision controls, building codes, etc.) before such permit may issue."[56]

Returning to the Fairfax County case, the second APF challenge was based on circumstances similar to the first. In *Board of Supervisors of Fairfax County v. Williams,*[57] the petitioner requested a zoning change on two tracts; the planning board had denied the request on the basis of highway, school, and sewage deficiencies. Despite the board's argument that its decision was consonant with the APF ordinance, the court found as a matter of fact that infrastructure capabilities were either presently available or would be in the reasonable future for this site.[58] This testimony neutralized the presumption of validity, forcing the county to carry the burden. Complementing this, the fact that two surrounding parcels were granted higher density uses established an arbitrary and capricious action on the board's part, forcing the court to find the ordinance invalid as applied.[59]

Despite these setbacks, the basic soundness of the APF ordinance was untouched. These challenges tested the *application of the ordinance, not the ordinance itself*. This reflects a comment mentioned earlier, that by articulating the criteria development is conditioned to, an adjudicative body is more fully able to assess board actions. The four Prince Georges and Fairfax County cases permitted the court to balance the board's decision against the reason assailed for denying the varied requests. This forced the board to justify its determinations, something which conventional zoning schemes do not require. Without this articulation, the standards for reviewing development applications are often hidden, not readily amenable to debate. A case where general constitutionality was the issue occurred in *Ramapo*.

This lack of articulated standards was evident in the *Ramapo* case. Following the adoption of Ramapo's phased growth plan, a landowner brought suit when permission to develop was denied, even though the existing zoning ordinances permitted the proposed single-family configurations. The plaintiff's failure to comply with the "special development permit" triggered litigation, calling upon the New York courts to scrutinize the validity of a zoning ordinance permitting residential development only in accordance with the sequential plan. In an unreported opinion,[60] Justice Galloway upheld the plan with the strongest presumption of validity. This was subsequently reversed in the appellate division,[61] only to be finally validated in New York's highest court, the court of appeals.[62] Specifically, the arguments in the appeal encompassed: that the ordinance's use of sequential controls was *ultra vires,* not within the state zoning enabling act; that the plan was exclusionary by placing an unreasonable restriction on the free mobility of the population; and that the technique constituted a taking of private property without just compensation. Regarding the *ultra vires* ruling, Justice Scileppi, writing the final opinion, remarked that while specific designation of sequential controls is not expressly authorized, "the additional inquiry remains as to whether the challenged amendments find their basis within the perimeters of the devices authorized and purposes sanctioned under enabling legislation . . . hence, unless we are to ignore the plain meaning of the statutory delegation, this much is clear: phased growth is well within the ambit of existing enabling legislation."[63]

Apparently enamored by the fact that the town had sustained its own citizen's protest to provide public housing,[64] the court discounted the exclusionary allegation. It reasoned that Ramapo asked not to be left alone, but rather than it be allowed to prevent the kind of deterioration that has infiltrated urban areas. Unfortunately, the court missed the point. The processes of urban deterioration do not singularly result from service inadequacies. Lack of services follows a more basic disinterest, a disinvestment in urban areas. Beyond the court's faulty analogy, the town's major commitment to low-income housing consisted of only 200 units, with 151 occupied by elderly whites. Of the 49 remaining units, less than 10 percent have black inhabitants.[65] More fundamentally, Ramapo is the epitome of an excessively restrictive system. As such, it is hard to rationalize this with the court's commendation of the plan.

Drawing upon the taking theory cited in *Arverne Bay Construction Company v. Thatcher,*[66] Ramapo's court reasoned that the numerable recourses available to affected landowners precluded confiscatory actions. This reasoning is very dubious. The reduced tax assessments allowed do not constitute any form of compensation, but merely are allowances for the fact that restrictions imposed have reduced the market value of the land, necessitating a realignment of assessments to reduce the harsh action: "Not only does the reduction in assessment value fail to compensate but it also fails as a mitigating factor of any sort, for the reduction is merely incidental to the dimunition in value."[67] The argument that the eighteen-year imposition is only a temporary restriction, since the property will eventually be put to a profitable use, is equally tenuous. This logic is impaired by a recent finding that even at the end of the program (1990), not all of the land in the town will qualify under the 15 point rating system.[68]

Despite the fact that some have heralded *Ramapo* as being the most significant zoning case since *Euclid,*[69] it is often overlooked that the case came up for only a summary judgement. This means that the basic facts went uncontroverted. The successful implementation of the eighteen-year capital improvement program was not challenged. In light of one study's findings that the phasing mechanism is not working,[70] other constitutional challenges to the Ramapo plan may arise in the future.

In the opinion expressed in *Ramapo,* the court placed heavy reliance on the town's comprehensive planning process. For this, Ramapo is to be commended. However, the notion that any planning automatically legitimizes an ordinance is nonsense. It is the spurious nature of this premise which will be examined in the next section in which we will attempt to develop an analytic approach to growth management. Previously articulated recommendations will be formulated in an effort to provide a generalized model.

NOTES

1. Stanford Environmental Law Society, *A Handbook for Controlling Local Growth* (Stanford, California: Stanford University, 1973), pp. 17-18.
2. 272 U.S. 365 (1926).
3. 260 U.S. 393 (1922).
4. "Tempo and Sequential Controls: The Validity of Attempts to Combat

Urban Sprawl Through Local Land Use Regulation," 11 *Willamette Law Journal* 217, 231 (1975).

5. Appeal of Kit-Mar Builders, Inc. 268 A. 2d 765 (1970).
6. National Land and Investment Company v. Kohn 215 A. 2d 597 (1965).
7. *Ibid.* at 612.
8. Southern Burlington County NAACP v. Township of Mt. Laurel 336 A. 2d 713 (1975).
9. Appeal of Girsh 263 A. 2d 395 (1970).
10. Township of Willistown v. Chesterdale Farms, Inc. 300 A. 2d 107 (1973).
11. In those states where this type of principle is promulgated, threatened single-family owners may possibly attempt to protect their area from intrusion of apartments by entering into restrictive covenants. See: Callahan v. Weiland 279 So. 2d 451 (1973) in which the Alabama Supreme Court held that such a restrictive provision is binding on the owner.
12. 192 N.W. 2d 322 (1971).
13. 507 P. 2d 23 (1973).
14. *Ibid.* at 28.
15. Jan Krasnowiecki, "Zoning Litigation: How To Win Without Really Losing," Unpublished paper, University of Pennsylvania Law School, Philadelphia, Pennsylvania, 1975, p. 7.
16. "The Right To Travel and Community Growth Controls," 12 *Harvard Journal on Legislation* 244, 245 (1975).
17. "The Right To Travel: Judicial Curiosity or Practical Tool?" 52 *Journal of Urban Law* 749, 752-755 (1975).
18. 275 F. Supp. 574 (1974).
19. *Ibid.* at 5.
20. *Ibid.* at 13.
21. 394 U.S. 618 (1968).
22. Crandall v. Nevada 73 U.S. 35 (1867); Edwards v. California 314 U.S. 160 (1941); Shapiro v. Thompson 394 U.S. 618 (1969); King v. New Rochelle Municipal Housing Authority 442 F. 2d 646 (1971); Cole v. Housing Authority 435 F. 2d 807 (1970); Dunn v. Blumstein 405 U.S. 330 (1972); Memorial Hospital v. Maricopa County 415 U.S. 250 (1974); but see, Sosha v. Iowa 95 S. Ct. 533 (1975) in which the court sustained a one-year residence requirement to obtain a divorce.
23. 405 U.S. 56 (1972).
24. *Ibid.* at 73-74.
25. "Towards A Recognition of a Constitutional Right to Housing," 42 *University of Missouri at Kansas City Law Review* 362, 373 (1974).
26. 415 U.S. 250 (1974).
27. *Ibid.* at 252.
28. Cole v. Housing Authority 435 F. 2d 807 (1970).
29. 442 F. 2d 646, 648 (1971).
30. "The Right To Travel: Another Constitutional Standard for Local Land Use Regulation?" 39 *University of Chicago Law Review* 612, 637 (1972).
31. "The Reconciliation of Land Use Laws and the Right to Travel: Toward a Realistic Standard of Judicial Review," 31 *Washington and Lee Law Review* 575 (1974).
32. *Ibid.* at 596-597.
33. Construction Industry Association of Sonoma County v. The City of Petaluma No. 74-2100, United States Court of Appeals for the Ninth Circuit, August 13, 1975, p. 11.
34. *Ibid.* at footnote 12.
35. David Moskowitz, "Standing of Future Residents in Exclusionary Zoning Cases," 6 *Akron Law Review* 189, 206 (1973).

36. Petaluma at 7.
37. *Ibid.* at 8.
38. _____ U.S. _____ _____ S. Ct. _____
39. *Petition For Rehearing and Suggestion for Hearing En Banc,* p. 3.
40. Richard Babcock, "On the Choice of Forum," 27 *Land Use Law and Zoning Digest* 8 (1975).
41. 437 F. 2d 1286 (1971).
42. *Ibid.* at 1288.
43. "Control of the Timing and Location of Government Utility Extensions," 26 *Stanford Law Review* 945, 951 (1974); and another, "Equal Protection as a Means of Securing Adequate Municipal Services," 1973 *Urban Law Annual* 277, 278 (1973).
44. Lawrence v. Richards 88 A. 2d. 92, 95 (1913).
45. "The Duty of a Public Utility to Render Adequate Service: Its Scope and Enforcement," 62 *Columbia Law Review* 312, 317 (1962).
46. Robinson v. Boulder 547 P. 2d 228 (1976).
47. Maryland National Capital Park and Planning Commission v. Rosenberg 307 A. 2d. 704, 707-709 (1973).
48. 198 N.Y.S. 2d 695, 699 (1960).
49. Docket Number 56854, Circuit Court of Prince Georges County.
50. *Ibid.* at 25.
51. Board of Supervisors of Fairfax County v. Allman, Record Numbers 730991 and 740029, Circuit Court of Fairfax County, January 30, 1975.
52. *Ibid.* at 2.
53. *Ibid.* at 15-16.
54. Jan Krasnowiecki, "Zoning Litigation and the New Pennsylvania Procedures," 120 *University of Pennsylvania Law Review* 1029, 1082 (1972), p. 1082.
55. 328 A. 2d 464 (1974).
56. *Ibid.* at 469. Further modification is offered in Ellick v. Board of Supervisors of Warchester Township 333 A. 2d 239 (1975).
57. Record Number 730996, Circuit Court of Fairfax County, June 13, 1975.
58. *Ibid.* at 3.
59. *Ibid.* at 16.
60. Unreported opinion. Golden v. Planning Board of the Town of Ramapo, New York. Index No. 525-1970.
61. 324 N.Y.S. 2d 178 (1971).
62. 285 N.E. 2d 291 (1972).
63. *Ibid.* at 4 and 8.
64. Farelly v. Town of Ramapo 317 N.Y.S. 2d 837 (1970); Greenwald v. Town of Ramapo 317 N.Y.S. 2d 839 (1970); and Fletcher v. Romney 323 F. Supp. 189 (1970).
65. Herbert Franklin, *"Controlling Urban Growth—But For Whom?"* (Washington, D.C.: Metropolitan Housing Program, Inc., 1973), p. 38 (footnote 15).
66. 15 N.E. 2d 587, 592 (1938).
67. "A Zoning Program For Phased Growth: Ramapo Township's Time Controls On Residential Development," 47 *New York University Law Review* 723, 754 at footnote 167 (1972).
68. National Association of Home Builders Task Force Trip to Ramapo, 1975, p. 9.

69. *Planning Magazine* 8/6 (Chicago: American Society of Planning Officials, 1972), pp. 108-109.
70. National Association of Homebuilders, *supra* 68, p. 9.

Section III
A Conceptual Approach

Section III
A Conceptual Approach: Model

The previous sections have attempted to explore the systemic elements of approximately twenty management techniques. Starting with conventional strategies and concluding with expanded applications, an effort has been made to articulate system advantages and disadvantages, linking each tool to a case study for illustrative purposes. Emerging from this process is a series of generalized conclusions:

1. Oftentimes a management program is viewed as a surrogate for comprehensive planning. It is not; there are many critical planning issues not addressed in growth management strategies alone.
2. While the prevention of sprawl is a commonly cited goal, this objective is seldom met due to programming facilities for low, and consequently dispersed, densities.
3. Frequently a regulation is adopted in response to a particular problem. This is unfortunate for isolating one element ignores the interdependency of the problems involved.
4. While rapid community growth is a major motivating factor for initiating a plan, few plans control all aspects of growth; most are content solely to regulate residential development.
5. While citizen pressures and concern over growth may have been an

underlying reason for enacting the program, few programs provide for continual citizen participation.

6. Oftentimes the growth control plan was superimposed on an already restrictive system.

7. While conventional approaches were criticized for their static nature, a growth control plan is not inherently any more dynamic, particularly in the absence of annual reviews.

8. While concern for the environment was an underlying rationale for adopting the program in most cases, virtually no plans took specific physiographic features into account; regulations were applied to all areas without regard to special features.

Based upon these observations, we have formulated a growth management model which allows for considerations of a community's fiscal, legal and infrastructure capacities, and its general goals. In the first run through, market forces predominate, yielding unconstrained growth potentials. System capabilities—in the form of infrastructure, fiscal, and legal limits—combined with local objectives—preserving rural character, preventing sprawl—would then be applied to the latter levels, producing a modified growth plan. An iterative procedure would then ensue until a version comprising the "best" elements of each was derived. Hopefully, through this union of opposites an acceptable compromise can be reached between both public and private goals.

The process might take place as follows. First, employment projections would be made using a shift-share or other moderately sophisticated technique. These forecasts could show employment potentials by sector, and applying average industry wage rates, an income profile of future workers could be constructed. Drawing on this employment and income data, population projections could be made possible by using a simple multiregression equation. Disaggregated by income, age, and household characteristics, a fairly solid understanding of the families buying property could be derived. This information could then be computed with current data on housing—occupancy patterns, type of stock, value—to determine housing demand. Housing demand data would then be qualified by market absorption potentials to determine annual housing pace by type, size, and unit value.

Similar analyses could be conducted for commercial and industrial facilities. Working from the employment projections, tempered with market information on price and yearly pace, the magnitude of these nonresidential uses could be determined. Aggregating the residential, commercial, and industrial paces, unconstrained land use demands could then be calculated. It is at this juncture that the management factors would be introduced.

Through a series of public meetings, citizen goals and objectives would be determined. Depending upon the outcome of these meetings, the next steps to be taken could be defined. Typically, concern for environmental factors can be partially mitigated by identifying sensitive lands—slopes, flood plains, and so

EXHIBIT VII

Conceptual Growth Management Model

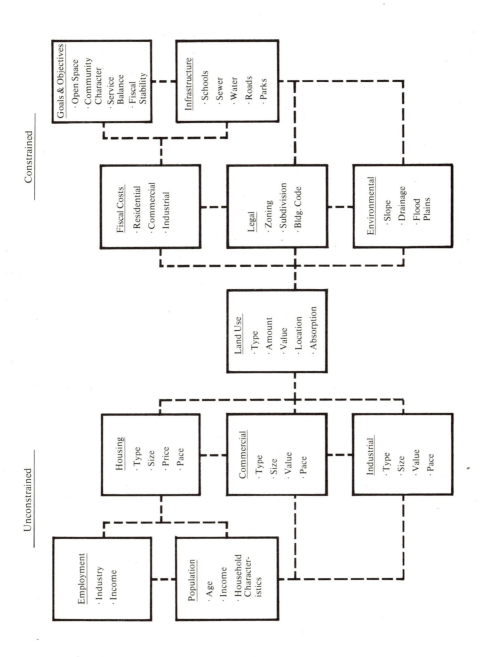

forth—and removing them from development activity. The previously determined annual land use projections could then be translated into infrastructure requirements and compared against existing capacity to determine the magnitude of any disparity. Then taking into account the fiscal and legal resources of the community—bonding ability, outstanding indebtedness—the unconstrained levels could be set in accordance with the community's ability to accommodate some amount of growth. However, it is crucial that the constraining factors developed by the community are realistic and not, as mentioned before, merely exclusionary veils. The advantages of such an approach are that it:

1. Reconstitutes the comprehensive planning process, growth management becomes an element of this process rather than growth management defining comprehensive planning;
2. Is multidimensional in that it takes into account the diversity of the area's socioeconomic future and is not based on one element;
3. Serves to update the master plan, providing data which could serve as inputs to other studies or funding requests; and
4. Is realistic in that market forces are recognized but qualified by the community's ability to assimilate growth.

The clash of demographic, fiscal, and environmental trends will define the context within which a management strategy is effectuated. The resolution of these issues will not be easy. It requires vast amounts of effort on the part of both public and private participants. It is hoped that this analysis has identified drawbacks in current undertakings, and has made some positive suggestions to help in achieving a balanced and equitable growth management system.

Bibliography

Though not exhaustive, the following listing represents a full complement of the materials specifically focusing on "newer" growth management techniques. While the majority of these citations address second generation programs, particularly notable articles illustrating conventional management uses or approaches have also been included.

General Books

1. Brower et al. *Urban Growth Management Through Development Timing.* Praeger Publishers, New York, New York. 1976.
2. Cranston et al. *A Handbook for Controlling Local Growth.* Stanford Environmental Law Society, Stanford University, Stanford, California. 1973.
3. Finkler, Earl, and David Peterson. *Nongrowth Planning Strategies: The Developing Power Of Towns, Cities and Regions.* Praeger Publishers, New York, New York. 1974.
4. Hughes, James W. (ed.). *Growth Controls.* Center for Urban Policy Research, Rutgers University, New Brunswick, New Jersey. 1974.

5. Peters, Terry S. *The Politics and Administration Of Land Use Control.* Lexington Books, Lexington, Massachusetts. 1974.
6. Reilly, William K. (ed.) *The Use Of Land: A Citizens' Policy Guide to Urban Growth.* Thomas Y. Crowell Company, New York, New York. 1973.
7. Scott, Randall W. (ed.). *Management and Control of Growth: Issues, Techniques, Problems, Trends.* Urban Land Institute, Washington, D.C. 1975.

General Articles

8. "Birth Control For Premature Subdivisions—A Legislative Pill." *Santa Clara Lawyer.* Volume 12, 1972, p. 523.
9. Bosselman, Fred P. "The Right To Move, The Need To Grow," *Planning Magazine.* American Society of Planning Officials. Chicago, Illinois. Volume 39, Number 8. 1973.
10. _____. "Growth Management and Constitutional Rights—Part I: The Blessings of Quiet Seclusion," *Urban Law Annual.* Volume 8, 1974, p. 3.
11. _____. "Can The Town Of Ramapo Pass A Law To Bind The Rights Of The Whole World?" *Florida State University Law Review. Volume 1,* 1974. p. 234.
12. Brooks, Mary E. "Mandatory Dedication Of Land Or Fees-In-Lieu of Land for Parks and Schools," *Planning Advisory Service.* American Society of Planning Officials. Chicago, Illinois. Report Number 266, 1971.
13. "Capital Improvement Programing—Some Considerations." *Planning Advisory Service.* American Society of Planning Officials, Chicago, Illinois. Report Number 23, 1951.
14. Carter et al. "Controlling Growth: A Challenge for Local Government." *The Municipal Yearbook.* Volume 41, 1974, p. 265.
15. Clark, Thomas P., Jr., and Roger A. Grable. "Growth Control In California: Prospects for Local Government Implementation of Timing and Sequential Control of Residential Development," *Pacific Law Journal.* Volume 5, 1974,
16. Cutler, Richard. "Legal and Illegal Methods For Controlling Community Growth On The Urban Fringe." *Wisconsin Law Review.* Volume 1, 1973, p. 56.
17. Elliot, Donald and Norman Marcus, "From Euclid to Ramapo: New Directions In Land Use Controls" *Hofstra Law Review.* Volume 1, 1973, p. 56.
18. Emanuel, Manuel S. "Ramapo's Managed Growth Program: A Close Look At Ramapo After Five Years." *Planners Notebook.* American Institute of Planners. Washington, D.C. Volume 4, Number 5, 1974.

19. Fagin, Henry. "Regulating The Timing Of Urban Development" *Law and Contemporary Problems.* Volume 20, Number 2, 1955. p. 298.
20. Finkler, Earl. "Nongrowth as a Planning Alternative: A Preliminary Examination of an Emerging Issue." *Planning Advisory Service.* American Society of Planning Officials. Chicago, Illinois. Report Number 283, 1972.
21. _____. "Nongrowth: A Review Of The Literature,"*Planning Advisory Service.* American Society of Planning Officials, Chicago, Illinois. Report Number 289, 1973.
22. Freilich, Robert H. "Development Timing, Moratoria, and Controlling Growth." *Institute On Planning, Zoning and Eminent Domain.* Southwestern Legal Foundation. Dallas, Texas. 1974, p. 147.
23. _____. "Golden v. Town of Ramapo: Establishing A New Dimension in American Planning Law." *Urban Lawyer.* Volume 4, 1972, p. IX.
24. _____. "Interim Development Controls: Essential Tools for Implementing Flexible Planning and Zoning." *Journal of Urban Law.* Volume 49, 1971, p. 65.
25. Freilich, Robert H., and John Ragsdale, Jr. "Timing and Sequential Controls—The Essential Basis For Effective Regional Planning: An Analysis of New Directions For Land Use Control In the Minneapolis—St. Paul Metropolitan Region." *Minnesota Law Review.* Volume 58, 1974, p. 1009.
26. Harvey, Robert O., and W.A.V. Clark, "Controlling Urban Growth: The New Zealand and Australian Experiment." *Appraisal Journal.* Volume 32, Number 4, 1964, p. 551.
27. Heeter, David. "Interim Zoning Ordinances." *Planning Advisory Service.* American Society of Planning Officials. Chicago, Illinois. Report Number 242, 1969.
28. Hughes, James W. "Suburbanization and Growth Controls." *The Annals of the American Academy of Political and Social Science.* Volume 422, 1975, p. 61.
29. Krasnowiecki, Jan F. *Zoning Litigation: How To Win Without Really Losing.* University of Pennsylvania Law School (unpublished). Philadelphia, Pennsylvania. 1975.
30. _____. "Zoning Litigation and the New Pennsylvania Procedure." *University of Pennsylvania Law Review.* Volume 120, 1972, p. 1029.
31. Krasnowiecki, Jan F. and James Paul. "The Preservation of Open Space in Metropolitan Areas." *University Of Pennsylvania Law Review.* Volume 101, *University of Pennsylvania Law Review.* Volume 120, 1972, p. 1029.
32. Krasnowiecki, Jan F., and Ann Strong. "Compensible Regulations For Open Space: A Means of Controlling Urban Growth." *Journal Of The American Institute of Planners.* Volume 29, Number 2, May, 1963, p. 88.
33. "Land Use Growth Controls: A Case Study of San Jose and Livermore, California." *Santa Clara Lawyer.* Volume 15, 1974, p. 1.

34. *Land Planning and Regulation of Development—III.* ALI-ABA Course of Study, Conference held in New Orleans, Louisiana, February, 1975.
35. Schmandt, Henry J. "Municipal Control of Urban Expansion." *Fordham Law Review.* Volume 29, 1961, p. 637.
36. "Phased Zoning: Regulation of the Tempo and Sequence of Land Development." *Stanford Law Review,* Volume 26, 1974, p. 585.
37. "Stop Gap and Interim Legislation: A Device to Maintain the Status Quo of an Area Pending the Adoption of a Comprehensive Zoning Ordinance or Amendment Thereto." *Syracuse Law Review.* Volume 18, 1967, p. 837.
38. "Subdivision Land Dedication: Objectives and Objections." *Stanford Law Review.* Volume 27, 1975, p. 419.
39. "Time Control, Sequential Zoning: The Ramapo Case." *Baylor Law Review.* Volume 25, 1973. p. 318.
40. "Time Controls On Land Use: Prophylactic Law For Planners." *Cornell Law Review.* Volume 57, 1972, p. 827.
41. Yearwood, Richard M. "Subdivision Law: Timing and Location Control." *Journal of Urban Law.* Volume 44, 1967, p. 585.
42. "Zoning Program For Phased Growth: Ramapo Township's Time Controls On Residential Development." *New York University Law Review.* Volume 47, 1972, p. 723.
43. Smith, Marlin R. "Does Petaluma Lie At The End Of The Road From Ramapo?" *Villanova Law Review.* Volume 19, 1974, p. 739.
44. "Tempo and Sequential Controls: The Validity of Attempts to Combat Urban Sprawl Through Local Land Use Regulation." *Willamette Law Journal.* Volume 11, 1975, p. 217.

Legal Analysis

45. "City Size Limitation: Municipal Government Attempts to Curtail Growth May Violate the Right to Travel." *Georgetown Law Journal.* Volume 60, 1972, p. 1363.
46. "Control Of The Timing And Location of Government Utility Extensions." *Stanford Law Review.* Volume 26, 1974, p. 945.
47. "Equal Protection As A Means Of Securing Adequate Municipal Services." *Urban Law Annual,* Volume 1973, 1973, p. 277.
48. Fessler, Daniel W., and Charles M. Haar. "Beyond the Wrong Side of the Tracks: Municipal Services in the Interstices of Procedures." *Harvard Civil Rights—Civil Liberties Law Review.* Volume 6, 1971, p. 441.
49. "Freedom of Travel and Exclusionary Land Use Regulations." *Yale Law Journal.* Volume 84, 1975, p. 1564.
50. The Evolution of Equal Protection—Education, Municipal Services and Welfare." *Harvard Civil Rights—Civil Liberties Law Review.* Volume 7, 1972, p. 104.

51. "The Duty of a Public Utility to Render Adequate Service: Its Scope and Enforcement." *Columbia Law Review.* Volume 62, 1962, p. 312.

52. "The Reconciliation of Land Use Laws and the Right to Travel: Toward A Realistic Standard of Judicial Review." *Washington and Lee Law Review.* Volume 31, 1974, p. 575.

53. "The Right to Travel and Community Growth Controls." *Harvard Journal of Legislation.* Volume 12, 1975, p. 244.

54. "The Right To Travel: Another Constitutional Standard For Local Land Use Regulation?" *University of Chicago Law Review.* Volume 39, 1972, p. 612.

55. Thomas, Norman C. "Public Utilities: Extension of Service." *Rutgers Law Review.* Volume 16, 1962, p. 318.

56. White, Michael D. "Water as a Tool in Land Use Control, Legal Considerations: An Exploratory Essay." *Rocky Mountain Mineral Law Institute.* Volume 20, 1975, p. 671.

Reports

57. Alesch, Daniel J. *Local Governments' Ability To Manage Growth In a Metropolitan Context.* The Rand Corporation. Santa Monica, California. Report Number P-5287 (for the National Science Foundation). 1974.

58. Alesch, Daniel J., and Robert A. Levine. *Growth in San Jose: A Summary Policy Statement.* The Rand Corporation. Santa Monica, California. Report Number R-1235 (for the National Science Foundation). 1973.

59. Bosselman, Fred P. *Alternatives to Urban Sprawl: Legal Guidelines for Governmental Action.* Prepared for the Consideration of the National Commission on Urban Problems. Research Report Number 15. Washington, D.C. 1975.

60. Clapp, James A. *Growth Management: Practices and Issues.* Prepared for the Assembly Committee on Local Government. San Diego State University. San Diego, California. 1975.

61. Chung, Hyung C. *Controlling The Rate Of Residential Growth: A Cost-Revenue Analysis for the Town of Ramapo, New York.* Final Report, 1971.

62. Downing, Donald A. *The Role of Water and Sewer Extension Financing in Guiding Urban Residential Growth.* Water Resources Center. University of Tennessee. Report Number 19. 1972.

63. Franklin, Herbert M. *Controlling Urban Growth—But for Whom? The Social Implications of Development Timing Controls.* The Potomac Institute, Inc. Washington, D.C. 1973.

64. Freilich, Robert H. *The Legal Basis for a Growth Control System in Fairfax County, Virginia.* PLUS Program Research Paper 2. Fairfax County, Virginia, 1973.

65. Gleeson et al. *Urban Growth Management Systems: An Evaluation of Policy Related Research.* American Society of Planning Officials. Chicago, Illinois. PAS Reports 309 and 310. 1975

66. Hayes, Gary G. *Institutional Alternatives for Providing Programmed Water and Sewer Services In Urban Growth Areas: A Case Study of Knoxville–Knox County, Tennessee.* Water Resources Center. University of Tennessee. Report Number 18. 1972.

67. *Impact of No-Growth Policies On Rehabilitation Production in Central Cities.* Urban Land Institute. Prepared for the Department of Housing and Urban Development. Washington, D.C. Report Number PB-232-285-1973.

68. Levine, Robert A. *Growth Control: Some Questions For Urban Decision Makers.* The Rand Corporation. Santa Monica, California. Report Number R-1419 (for the National Science Foundation). 1974.

69. *Local Growth Management Policy: A Legal Primer.* The Potomac Institute, Inc. Washington, D.C., 1975.

70. Metropolitan Council of the Twin Cities Area. *Development Framework Report: Legal Study of the Control of Urban Sprawl in the Minneapolis-St. Paul Metropolitan Region.* Minneapolis-St. Paul, Minnesota. 1974.

71. Morrison, Peter A. *Guiding Urban Growth: Policy Issues and Demographic Constraints.* The Rand Corporation. Santa Monica, California. Report Number P-5212. 1974.

72. *Report of the National Association of Home Builders' Task Force Field Trip to Ramapo, New York.* National Association of Home Builders. Washington, D.C. 1975.

73. Rivkin/Carson, Inc. *The Sewer Moratorium as a Technique of Growth Control and Environmental Protection.* Prepared for the Department of Housing and Urban Development. Washington, D.C. Report Number H-2095. 1973.

74. Aurora, Colorado. *A Report on Population Growth in the City of Aurora.* Planning Department, Aurora, Colorado. 1975.

75. Boca Raton, Florida. *Emergency Ordinance Number 1756. Charter Amendment Partial Building Moratorium Ordinance.* Adopted November 8, 1972, Boca Raton, Florida.

76. Boulder, Colorado. *Exploring Options For the Future: A Study of Growth in Boulder County.* Boulder Area Growth Study Commission. Boulder, Colorado. 1973.

77. Brooklyn Park, Minnesota. *Development of Lands North of 85th Avenue in Brooklyn Park, Minnesota.* Planning Department, Brooklyn Park, Minnesota. 1972.

78. Dade County, Florida. *Ordinance Number 72-18.* Concerning moratoriums on issuance of building permits. 1972.

79. Eugene-Springfield, Oregon. *1990 Plan, Eugene–Springfield Metropolitan Area.* Lane Council of Governments. Eugene, Oregon. 1972.

80. Fairfax County, Virginia. *Proposal for Implementing an Improved Planning and Land Use Control System in Fairfax County.* Final Report of the Task Force on Comprehesive Planning and Land Use Control. Fairfax County, Virginia. 1973.
81. Loudoun County, Virginia. *Zoning Ordinance—As Amended.* Loudoun County, Virginia. 1972.
82. Manatee County, Florida. *A Policy to Encourage Optimum Population and Urban Growth In Manatee County, Florida.* Bradenton, Florida. 1972.
83. Montgomery County, Maryland. *Interim Report of the Advisory Committee on County Growth Policy for Montgomery County, Maryland.* National Capital Park and Planning Commission. Silver Spring, Maryland. 1974.
84. Milpitas, California. *History and Evaluation of the 1971-1972 Local Government Structure Study.* Planning Department. Milpitas, California. 1972.
85. Minneapolis-St. Paul, Minnesota. *Development Framework Chapter, Metropolitan Development Guide.* Metropolitan Council, Minneapolis, Minnesota. 1975.
86. Palo Alto, California. *Foothills Environmental Design Study.* Livingston and Blayney. San Francisco, California. 1970.
87. Petaluma, California. *Environmental Design Plans.* Department of Commuity Development. Petaluma, California. 1973.
88. Pleasanton, California. *Pleasanton General Plan Review: Alternative Growth Policies.* Livingston and Blayney. San Francisco, California. 1972.
89. Pinellas County, Florida. *Pinellas County Building Permit Allocation Program.* County Administrator. Pinellas County, Florida. 1974.
90. Pitkin County, Colorado. *Pitkin County Growth Management Plan-Draft.* Aspen-Pitkin Planning Board. Aspen, Colorado. 1975.
91. Prince Georges County, Maryland. *Proposed Staging Policy For Prince Georges County.* County Council. Prince Georges County, Maryland. 1973.
92. Ramapo, New York. *Development Plan For The Town of Ramapo: Background Studies, Proposed Plan and Effectuation.* Planning Board. Ramapo, New York. 1966.
93. Sacramento County, California. *Preliminary General Plan, Appendix I. Economic Analysis: To Guide the Physical Growth of Sacramento County to 1990.* Planning Department. Sacramento County, California. 1972.
94. Salem, Oregon. *Resolutions 74-103 and 74-112* concerning annexation and service policies of the City of Salem. Salem, Oregon. 1974.
95. San Jose, California. *Urban Development Policies—City of San Jose, California.* Planning Department. San Jose, California. 1972.